THE GAME COOKBOOK

THE
GAME
COOKBOOK

Colin Brown

SOUVENIR PRESS

First published in Australia by
Methuen Australia Pty Ltd.

First British Edition published 1986 by
Souvenir Press Ltd., 43 Great Russell Street London WC1B 3PA

ISBN 0 285 62768 6

A Shoal Bay Press book
Photography by Robert A.F. Van de Voort

Printed in Hong Kong

CONTENTS

TROUT

SALMON

VENISON

HARE

RABBIT

WILD BOAR

GOAT

DUCK

GOOSE

PHEASANT

QUAIL

PIGEON

GUINEA FOWL

PARTRIDGE

GROUSE

SNIPE

WOODCOCK

AUTHOR'S NOTE

As a chef I have my share of cookbooks, and each time I've added to my collection I have become aware of the relative scarcity of books devoted to game cookery or, indeed, of game recipes in general cookbooks. My restaurant specialises in game food, so over the years I have experimented with new dishes and combinations and built up my own collection of recipes. I hope this selection will provide new ideas to the seasoned game cook and some inspiration to those who have yet to discover the wonderful potential of game food.

There is a certain romance in the tradition of hunting and killing one's own food. This is tempered in most places by strict laws governing what may or may not be taken and when. These laws are framed to ensure conservation of the species and should always be strictly observed.

Those fortunate enough to have access to freshly-killed game will have whole animals available. I have attempted to provide recipes for as many cuts as possible so that nothing need be wasted. Fortunately the 'famine or feast' predicament of the primitive hunter can be avoided these days because game freezes well. Prepare it as you would before cooking and pack it in air-tight bags, clearly labelled and dated. Game birds and meat will keep for up to six months, and fish for up to three. After these times flavour and texture begin to deteriorate.

Many of us, however, will resort to selecting our own cuts from supermarket or butcher as game becomes more readily available through retail outlets.

This highlights one of the challenges of writing about game cookery — the uncertainty about the quality of the main ingredient of the recipe. A wild beast or bird will take on the hue of its environment and the taste of its flesh may vary slightly from place to place, according to the animal's diet. Factors of age, size and condition will always be relevant. Game reared commercially will be more reliable as to texture and tenderness but it will almost certainly have a milder flavour than its wild counterpart and may lack the superb leanness of an animal forced to fend for itself.

So a certain amount of flexibility is required of the cook, who should be prepared to adjust cooking times, if necessary, to achieve a tender result. One or two other observations about my recipes.

Measurements are given in metric and imperial figures. These will not be exact equivalents but if you operate in one system or the other you will achieve the correct proportions. Again, you may need to exercise your discretion in length of cooking time if your piece of meat is larger or smaller than that specified.

Thermostats do vary from oven to oven so use your own experience to adjust the temperatures given if you consider it necessary. It is important to pre-heat your oven before using it, as the initial heat can be quite fierce.

Throughout the recipes I have not specified any particular type of cooking oil. My own preference would be for olive oil or peanut oil, but any fresh, good quality oil will be adequate. Similarly, use whatever wine happens to be in your cupboard, provided it is dry and of reasonably good quality. (If you wouldn't drink the stuff yourself it won't do!)

Always try to use stock in preference to water. If you make a habit of boiling up leftover bones and trimmings with a few vegetables to make a simple stock, it will keep well in the freezer and can be readily thawed for use in sauces and gravies.

Finally, don't be afraid to experiment. The various stuffings and sauces are listed individually in the index and you might hit upon an exciting new combination of tastes for yourself by substituting one for another.

I have tried to keep the recipes relatively simple, not only for ease of preparation but because game's delicate and interesting flavours are too often obscured by over-fussy additions. The same can be said for the vegetables you choose to serve. Occasionally I have included suggestions for accompanying dishes, most often where these are a traditional part of the meal itself. Otherwise I suggest you choose simply prepared, seasonal vegetables to complement each dish.

Game dresses up superbly but it need not be kept just for special occasions; it can be a delicious, practical and welcome addition to the family menu.

COLIN BROWN

TROUT

FISHING SEASON
England/Wales: 1st March-31st October
Scotland: 15th March-6th October

Trout is a fine game fish which is also highly prized for its flesh and flavour. Brown trout, which are indigenous to the lakes and rivers of Europe, North Africa and North West Asia, have also been introduced to many other countries. They are very speckled and vary in colour from greenish brown to almost black. Once out of the water they become silvery. They commonly weigh between 225 g-1.4 kg (8 oz-3 lb).

Rainbow trout, with their star-shaped speckled markings, are more suitable for fish farming than brown trout. They generally weigh between 225-450 g (8 oz-1 lb).

Fresh trout should be cleaned and cooked on the day of purchase. It is important to note that fish requires very little cooking time and preparation should be organised so that the trout can be served as soon as they are cooked. Use the times given as a guide, but test the trout to see if they are done by touching the flesh gently — if it yields to pressure it is cooked.

Smoked trout is a special delicacy which should be served no more elaborately than with a twist of lemon and a slice of brown bread and butter.

Stuffed Trout

TIME TO ALLOW: 1 hour
SERVES 6

6 trout, each about 8 ounces (200 g)
1 ounce (25 g) of each of the following:
   green olives, sweet pimento, almonds, mushrooms
seasoning
⅛ pint (75 ml) oil
⅛ pint (75 ml) vinegar
breadcrumbs
1 clove garlic, crushed

Clean the trout and season with salt, pepper and a squeeze of lemon juice.

Chop the olives, pimento, almonds and mushrooms and season with salt and pepper, oil, and vinegar. Mix thoroughly, place the stuffing inside the cavities of the trout and secure with toothpicks. Rub each trout with oil and breadcrumbs, then roll them up in sheets of lightly-greased greaseproof paper.

Place the fish on a baking tray and bake in a moderately hot oven (400°F/205°C/gas regulo 5) until cooked — about 15-20 minutes.

Serve the trout in the paper.

Blue Trout

This is a classic preparation, but it will only be successful when the trout are really fresh.

TIME TO ALLOW: 40 minutes
SERVES 6

6 trout, each about 8 ounces (200 g)
3 pints (2 litres) water
½ pint (300 ml) white vinegar
1 large onion, peeled and sliced
1 large carrot, peeled and sliced
2 bay leaves
2 sticks celery
8 black peppercorns
small bunch of parsley stalks
salt

Prepare the stock by combining all the ingredients, except the trout, in a large braising dish. Bring to the boil and simmer very gently for 20 minutes.

Sprinkle the trout with a little vinegar and plunge them into the stock, cooking as quickly as possible, about 10-12 minutes in all.

Drain and serve with hollandaise sauce or melted butter.

Blue trout may also be served cold, in which case they are allowed to cool in the stock.

Poached Trout with Fennel Sauce

TIME TO ALLOW: 15 minutes
SERVES 6

6 trout, each about 8 ounces (200 g)
½ pint (300 ml) white wine
½ pint (300 ml) cream
1 ounce (25 g) fresh fennel, chopped
seasoning

Pour the wine and cream in to a large frying pan and place the trout fillets in. (If the fillets do not fit lying flat, they can be rolled.) Season, and cover with a lid. Bring the sauce to the boil on a reasonably high heat and continue to boil for a further 2 minutes. Remove the trout to a serving dish and keep warm.

Return the pan to the element and add the fennel. Correct the seasoning. Simmer the sauce gently until the volume is reduced by about one-third, when it should be of a nice coating consistency. Pour the sauce over the trout.

This is not an entirely orthodox method of poaching, but it works well, and all the flavour from the trout remains in the sauce. Above all else, it is simple.

Trout Poached in Red Wine

TIME TO ALLOW: 30-45 minutes
SERVES 6

6 trout, each about 8 ounces (200 g)
1 ounce (25 g) butter
1 medium onion, chopped finely
1 bay leaf,
dry red wine to cover
1 ounce (25 g) cornflour, mixed with a little cold water
pinch of sugar
seasoning

Choose a baking dish large enough to accommodate the trout, and grease with butter. Put the trout, finely chopped onions and bay leaf in the dish, cover with the red wine and season. Cover the dish with buttered paper and poach the trout in a slow oven (300°F/145°C/gas regulo 1) for about 15 minutes, until they are tender but still firm. Lay the trout on a dry cloth or kitchen towel and carefully remove the skins. Arrange them on a serving dish and keep warm.

Bring the red wine poaching liquor to the boil, season to taste, add a pinch of sugar and thicken with the cornflour and water solution. Spoon over the trout and serve.

Trout and Rice Salad

TIME TO ALLOW: 30 minutes
SERVES 6

6 trout, each about 8 ounces (200 g)
½ pint (300 ml) water
½ pint (300 ml) white wine
1 pound (450 g) cooked long-grain rice
1 red pimento, seeded and chopped
1 medium onion, chopped finely
4 ounces (100 g) green peas, cooked and chilled
⅛ pint (75 ml) white vinegar
¼ pint (150 ml) oil
juice from 1 lemon
seasoning

Poach the trout in the wine and water for about 10 minutes, and while still warm, remove the skins and bones. Flake the trout and mix with the rice, pimento, onion and peas. Season to taste, then add the vinegar and lemon juice. Lastly, add the oil and mix lightly.

Taste to correct the seasoning, and serve dressed on red lettuce with lemon garnishes.

Trout Fried in Oatmeal

TIME TO ALLOW: 30 minutes
SERVES 6

6 trout, each about 8 ounces (200 g)
10 ounces (250 g) coarse oatmeal
½ pint (300 ml) milk
oil
seasoning

Fillet the trout, making a total of 12 fillets, and pat them dry with a kitchen towel. Dip the fillets in milk and cover with oatmeal. Pan-fry in oil until nicely browned — about 3 minutes on each side.

Season and serve with a simple garnish of lemon wedges and parsley.

Steamed Trout with Mushrooms

TIME TO ALLOW: 30 minutes
SERVES 6

6 trout, each about 8 ounces (200 g)
8 ounces (200 g) mushrooms, preferably button
1 clove garlic, crushed
3 spring onions, chopped
¼ pint (150 ml) peanut oil
⅛ pint (75 ml) soya sauce
⅛ pint (75 ml) white wine
seasoning

Place the cleaned trout in a large dish with the sliced mushrooms. Combine the garlic and spring onions with the oil, soya sauce, wine and seasoning. Mix well and pour over the trout.

Place the dish in a steamer (or a large roasting dish with a wire rack over rapidly boiling water). Cover and steam for about 10 minutes, or until the trout are tender. Remove and serve immediately.

Sautéed Trout with Orange Sauce

TIME TO ALLOW: 30 minutes
SERVES 6

6 trout, each about 8 ounces (200 g)
4 ounces (100 g) butter
1/8 pint (75 ml) Grand Marnier (or other orange liqueur)
1/8 pint (75 ml) brandy
juice from 1 orange
1/2 pint (300 ml) cream
1 ounce (25 g) chives, chopped
flour
seasoning

Melt the butter in a heavy-bottomed frying pan and add the trout which have been dusted with flour. Season, and brown evenly, without letting the pan become too hot.

When the trout are cooked (about 15 minutes) remove to a serving dish and keep warm.

Add the brandy and Grand Marnier to the pan and set alight. It is important not to have the pan too hot, or the resultant flames will be too fierce. As the flames die down add the orange juice and cream. Taste to correct the seasoning, then allow the sauce to reduce in volume by simmering gently for about 5 minutes. Just before serving, add the chives and pour the sauce over the trout.

Sautéed Trout with Almonds

TIME TO ALLOW: 30 minutes
SERVES 6

6 trout, each about 8 ounces (200 g)
4 ounces (100 g) butter
4 ounces (100 g) slivered almonds
juice of half a lemon
small bunch parsley, washed and chopped finely
milk
flour
seasoning

Season the cleaned trout with salt and freshly ground black pepper. Dip them into milk, then in flour, and sauté in half the butter until evenly browned on both sides. Add the remaining butter and the slivered almonds and continue to cook, browning the almonds. When the fish are just cooked, add the lemon juice and parsley and stir in. Spoon the sauce over the trout before serving.

Rainbow Trout with Lemon

TIME TO ALLOW: 30 minutes
SERVES 6

6 trout, each about 8 ounces (200 g)
4 ounces (100 g) butter
juice of 1 lemon
¼ pint (150 ml) white wine
seasoning
chopped parsley

Melt the butter in a heavy-bottomed frying pan and fry the trout on a moderate heat until golden brown — about 7-8 minutes on each side. Add the lemon juice, then the white wine and season. Cook for a further 2 minutes then remove the trout to serving plates and keep warm.

Add the chopped parsley to the pan juices and taste to correct seasoning. Spoon over the trout before serving.

Pan-fried Trout with Capers

TIME TO ALLOW: 30 minutes
SERVES 6

6 trout, each about 8 ounces (200 g)
2 ounces (50 g) butter
2 ounces (50 g) flour
juice from 1 lemon
1 ounce (25 g) capers
seasoning

Dust the trout with flour and melt the butter in a heavy-bottomed frying pan. Brown the trout evenly for about 6 minutes on each side. Season, then add the lemon juice and capers to the pan juices and continue cooking for a further 2-3 minutes. Spoon the caper sauce over the trout to serve.

Crumbed Pan-fried Trout

TIME TO ALLOW: 30 minutes
SERVES 6

6 trout, each about 8 ounces (200 g)
seasoning
flour
egg wash
breadcrumbs
oil for frying

Fillet, and skin and bone the trout, making 12 fillets in all. (Use clean pliers to remove the small bones.)

Pass the trout fillets through the seasoned flour, egg-wash and breadcrumbs.

Heat some oil in a heavy-bottomed frying pan and pan-fry the fillets until golden on each side, about 10 minutes in all. Drain the fillets on kitchen paper and serve with lemon wedges, and perhaps sauce rémoulade.

Very simply prepared and quite delicious.

Crumbed, pan-fried trout

SALMON

FISHING SEASON
England/Wales/Scotland: 1st February-31st October

Like any other fish, salmon must be very fresh to get the best results. It should have bright eyes, firm flesh with bright silvery scales and very red gills, and have a light but not unpleasant fishy smell. A mature salmon usually weighs about 4-5 kg (10 lb) and a grilse (a young salmon) between 1.7-3.6 kg (4-8 lb).

A big salmon, cooked and served whole, is a magnificent centrepiece for any culinary occasion. It is better to err on the side of undercooking so that the salmon remains firm and moist.

Often the simplest preparations are the best; salmon's delicate flavour can be easily overwhelmed by too rich a sauce or too fanciful a side dish.

Chilled poached salmon (p.29)

Sautéed Salmon with Mange-tout Peas

TIME TO ALLOW: 30 minutes
SERVES 6

6 slices salmon, each about 6 ounces (150 g)
6 ounces (150 g) mange-tout peas
2 ounces (50 g) butter
1 tablespoon oil
¼ pint (150 ml) white wine
flour
seasoning

Season the salmon slices and dust with flour. Heat a heavy-bottomed frying pan and melt the butter with the oil. When hot, add the salmon and brown on both sides. Add the trimmed mange-tout peas and cook for about 10 minutes, or until the salmon is almost cooked. Add the wine and cook for a further 3-5 minutes.

Remove the salmon to a serving dish and spoon the sauce over to serve.

Sautéed Salmon with Gherkins

TIME TO ALLOW: 30 minutes
SERVES 6

6 slices salmon, each about 6 ounces (150 g)
2 ounces (50 g) butter
4 ounces (100 g) gherkins, cut into strips
juice from half a lemon
¼ pint (150 ml) white wine
flour
seasoning

Season the salmon slices and dust with flour. Heat a heavy-bottomed frying pan and melt the butter. When the pan is hot add the salmon and cook until golden on both sides, 5-6 minutes for each side. Add the gherkins and lemon, then the wine. Bring to the boil and taste to correct the seasoning.

Remove the salmon to serving plates and spoon the sauce over before serving.

Pan-fried Salmon with Sesame Seeds

TIME TO ALLOW: 30 minutes
SERVES 6

6 slices fresh salmon, each about 6 ounces (150 g)
2 ounces (50 g) sesame seeds, lightly toasted
1 ounce (25 g) butter
6 drops sesame oil
oil
seasoning
flour
milk
juice from half a lemon

Melt the butter in a heavy-bottomed frying pan and add a little oil and
the sesame oil. Mix half the sesame seeds with a little flour. Dip the salmon
into milk and then into the flour and sesame seed mixture. Shake off excess
seeds, season, and pan-fry the salmon until done, about 5-6 minutes on
each side.

Remove the salmon to a serving tray, then add the remainder of the
sesame seeds to the pan. Add the lemon juice and a touch of water, bring
to the boil, season, and pour over the salmon.

Braised Salmon on a Bed of Vegetables

TIME TO ALLOW: 1-1½ hours
SERVES 8 to 10

1 salmon, about 8 pounds (4 kg)
2 medium onions, sliced
3 medium carrots, peeled and sliced
3-4 small courgettes, sliced on an angle
1 green pepper, seeded and sliced
1 pint (600 ml) white wine
small bunch parsley, chopped finely
seasoning
oil
flour

Slice all the vegetables neatly and place them in an oven dish large enough to take the salmon. Season and add a little oil. Cook the vegetables in a moderate oven (375°F/190°C/gas regulo 4) for about 10-15 minutes, then remove the dish, sprinkle a little flour on the vegetables, then place the salmon on top. Add the wine which should come to about halfway up the salmon. Cover the dish with a lid or foil and braise in a moderate oven until the salmon is cooked — about 30-40 minutes depending on size.

Remove from the oven and carefully lift the salmon from the dish to a flat serving tray. (You will need two fish slices and a great deal of care!) Peel the skin from the salmon.

Taste to correct the seasoning of the vegetables and surround the salmon with them.

Chilled Poached Salmon with Cucumber and Dill Salad

TIME TO ALLOW: 3 hours (including cooling)
SERVES 6

1 salmon about 3 pounds (1.5 kg), (cleaned and gutted but not skinned)
½ pint (300 ml) white wine
2 bay leaves
1 medium onion, sliced
8 black peppercorns
2 lemons, halved
salt
water
parsley stalks

3 medium cucumbers
6 sprigs fresh dill, chopped
½ pint (300 ml) sour cream
seasoning

In a large dish suitable for element or gas cooking, place white wine, bay leaves, peppercorns, onion, lemons and parsley stalks. Place salmon (whole) into it, add cold water until nearly ⅔ up the salmon. Season with salt and cover tightly with lid or foil. Bring slowly to the boil, then remove from the heat and allow to cool in cooking liquor.

Meanwhile, peel cucumbers, halve lengthways and scoop the pips from the middle. Sprinkle with salt and allow to stand a while. Slice cucumbers and mix with chopped dill, season lightly with a little extra salt, freshly ground white pepper and a pinch of sugar. Blend in sour cream, correct seasoning.

Remove the salmon carefully from the cooking dish and place on a serving tray. Peel the skin off gently, taking care not to damage the flesh. Decorate with a suitable garnish and serve.

See photograph opposite p.25

Poached Salmon with Dill Sauce

TIME TO ALLOW: 20 minutes
SERVES 6

6 slices salmon fillet, each about 6 ounces (150 g)
½ pint (300 ml) white wine
½ pint (300 ml) cream
2 ounces (50 g) fresh dill, chopped
seasoning

Place the salmon in a large pan and add the wine and cream. Season and cover with a lid. Cook on a moderately high heat and by the time the liquor is boiling the salmon will be virtually cooked. Remove the salmon when done to a serving tray and keep warm while preparing the sauce.

Taste to correct the seasoning then return the sauce to the boil until it has reduced by about a third in volume. Add the dill and correct the consistency of the sauce, then coat the salmon with the dill sauce.

Grilled Salmon Steaks with Tomato

TIME TO ALLOW: 30 minutes
SERVES 6

6 salmon steaks, each about 7-8 ounces (175-200 g)
2 large tomatoes, skinned
6 small leaves fresh basil
oil
seasoning

Season the salmon steaks and brush with oil. Peel the tomatoes (cut a cross in the top of each and remove the core, then plunge it into boiling water for 7-10 seconds. The skin will come off quite easily). Slice the tomatoes thinly, then place a leaf of basil and 2-3 slices of tomato on top of each salmon steak. Brush with a little more oil and season to taste.

Cook under the grill until the salmon is cooked through, about 10-12 minutes.

Grilled Spicy Salmon

TIME TO ALLOW: 3 hours for marinating; 20 minutes for cooking
SERVES 6

6 slices salmon fillet, each about 6 ounces (150 g)
¼ pint (150 ml) olive oil
juice from 1 lemon
2 red chillis, sliced finely
1 medium onion, sliced finely
salt
freshly ground black pepper

Mix the olive oil, lemon juice, chillis and onion together, adding salt and black pepper. Rub the salmon with this mixture and leave to marinate for 2⅛-3 hours, turning the salmon on the hour.

Place the salmon on a tray and rub with any remaining marinade. Grill until the salmon is cooked, about 15 minutes.

Choron sauce, which is a hollandaise mixed with a little tomato purée, is delicious with spicy salmon.

Marinated Salmon

TIME TO ALLOW: 20 minutes for preparation, overnight marinating
SERVES 6 to 8

2 pounds (1 kg) fresh salmon fillets
5 ounces (125 g) salt
3 ounces (75 g) sugar
20 white peppercorns
large bunch of fresh dill

There are several preparations of salmon in this style, but this is the one which I find most successful.

Leaving the skin on, remove the bones from the fillets of salmon. (Pliers are most useful for this job.)

Place a thick layer of fresh dill in a deep dish. Crush the peppercorns and mix with the salt and sugar. Rub the salmon with some of this mixture and sprinkle some on top of the dill. Place the salmon, skin side down on top of the dill. Place a layer of dill on top and sprinkle with a little more of the salt mixture. Place the next fillet skin side up so the thicker (head) end of the fillet meets the thinner (tail) end of the other salmon fillet. Place more dill on top and a sprinkling of the salt blend.

Cover with a tight-fitting plate or something similar that fits into the dish and put a heavy weight on it to press the salmon. Leave to stand for about a day (overnight for the next evening is best), turning a few times.

When you are ready to serve the salmon, scrape off the seasoning and slice thinly on an angle towards the tail. Serve with a few capers, a fresh sprig of dill and some lemon wedges.

Creamed Salmon au Gratin

TIME TO ALLOW: 45 minutes
SERVES 8

2 pounds (1 kg) cooked salmon with skin and bones removed
1 medium onion, chopped finely
1 ounce (25 g) butter
1 ounce (25 g) flour
¾ pint (450 ml) milk, scalded
seasoning
4 ounces (100 g) grated cheese

Fry the onion in a saucepan in the butter until it is clear but not coloured. Add the flour and cook for a few minutes. Allow to cool then add the scalded milk, stirring constantly to avoid lumps. Season and bring to the boil.

Add the flaked cooked salmon and taste to correct the seasoning. A pinch of nutmeg will give an interesting flavour. Pour the mixture into an ovenproof dish and sprinkle with the grated cheese. Glaze under the grill.

Hot Salmon Mousse

TIME TO ALLOW: 1 hour
SERVES 8

2 pounds (1 kg) fresh salmon, skinned and boned
1 medium onion, chopped finely
small bunch of fresh dill, chopped
2 egg whites
oil
seasoning
8 large lettuce leaves
½ pint (300 ml) cream

Mince or chop the salmon finely. Add the onion and dill and season. Mix lightly, then add the egg whites, continuing to blend.

Choose 8 of the larger outside leaves of a lettuce. If they are too crisp, run them under hot water to make them more pliable. Divide the mixture evenly between the 8 leaves. Place the mix on each half and roll up neatly.

Rub a heavy pan with oil and place in the salmon in lettuce. Season lightly and add the cream. Bring slowly to the boil and simmer for about 10 minutes until cooked.

Salmon en Brochette

TIME TO ALLOW: 30 minutes for marinating, 15 minutes for cooking
SERVES 6

2 pounds (1 kg) fresh salmon, skinned and boned
½ pint (300 ml) oil
juice from 1 lemon
small bunch parsley, chopped
seasoning
8 ounces (200 g) button mushrooms

Cut the salmon into cubes and marinate with the oil, lemon juice, parsley and a little seasoning. Leave for 30 minutes then thread the salmon on skewers alternating with the mushrooms. This should yield 6 good-size portions.

Place on a tray and grill until done — about 10 minutes.

A lemon and parsley sauce would be appropriate for this dish. Serve the brochettes on a bed of rice and pour the sauce over.

Mixed Salmon Salad

TIME TO ALLOW: 30 minutes
SERVES 8

2 pounds (1 kg) cooked salmon, skinned and boned
1 large onion, peeled and sliced
1 cucumber, peeled, de-seeded and sliced
2 tomatoes, cored and cut in wedges
8 celery shoots
1 ounce (25 g) sunflower seeds
½ pint (300 ml) prepared mayonnaise
⅛ pint (75 ml) white vinegar
¼ pint (150 ml) oil
seasoning

Flake the salmon and combine with all the other ingredients except the mayonnaise, vinegar and oil. Season. Mix the mayonnaise, vinegar and oil together and add to the salmon. Taste to correct the seasoning and serve either as an appetiser or as a main dish, dressed on fresh spinach leaves.

VENISON

Venison is the flesh of deer — a lean dark red meat with a fine grain and a distinctive flavour. The longer it is hung, or marinated, the more pronounced will be the taste. Rub over with a mixture of flour and pepper and hang in a cool, well-aired, insect-free place for four to five days. Run a fine skewer into the haunch, close to the bone, to test whether it is ready to use or not. If the skewer comes out clean it is in prime condition. The flesh should have a slightly gamey, but not musty, smell.

The leg or the saddle are the prime cuts for roasting. They can be served whole, hot or cold, at a large function, or in smaller pieces for family eating. They should always be slightly underdone, pink and moist. The saddle can be divided into fillet or loin or rib chops for grilling. The shoulder can be roasted or braised whole, or cut into pieces for stewing. The flank and neck need long, slow cooking and the shins and shank are best reserved for sausages, pâté or stock.

Venison is available frozen all the year round; fresh venison is only available in the open season which varies according to species, sex and region.

Venison Stock

TIME TO ALLOW: 3-4 hours

2 pounds (1 kg) raw bones
2 pints (1200 ml) water
8 ounces (200 g) vegetables (carrot, onion, celery, leek)
1 bay leaf
6 peppercorns

Chop the bones, cover with cold water and bring to the boil. If the scum is dirty discard the water, wash the bones and re-cover with cold water. Return to the boil, add the other ingredients and simmer gently for 3-4 hours. It may be necessary to top up the stock with cold water during the simmering. Skim the stock and then strain.

Venison and Lentil Broth

TIME TO ALLOW: 2 hours (from prepared stock)
SERVES 6

8 ounces (200 g) lentils
2 pints (1200 ml) stock
2 ounces (50 g) diced, cooked venison
2 ounces (50 g) onion, chopped
2 ounces (50 g) carrot, chopped
⅛ pint (75 ml) cream

Cook the lentils in lightly seasoned stock with the onion and carrot until soft, about 1-1½ hours. Pass through a sieve into a clean pot, add the venison, bring back to the boil and correct the seasoning. Lastly, stir in the cream and serve.

Venison Consommé

TIME TO ALLOW: 4 hours (from prepared stock)
SERVES 6

2 pints (1200 ml) venison stock
8 ounces (200 g) minced raw venison
1 medium onion, diced finely
1 stick celery, diced finely
1 bay leaf
6 peppercorns
4 parsley stalks
2 egg whites
⅛ pint (75 ml) dry sherry
seasoning

Prepare the stock (opposite) and allow to cool. When the stock is completely cold, mix in all the other ingredients except the sherry and seasoning. Bring gradually to the boil, stirring all the time. Move the pot to the side of the element and simmer very gently for 3-4 hours without further stirring. The mince should come together, and with it, the impurities.

After 3-4 hours' simmering the soup should be perfectly clear. Strain it through a muslin cloth that has been rinsed in cold water. (This helps the fat to stay in the cloth rather than to go into the consommé.)

Check the seasoning and adjust accordingly. Pour in the sherry and serve.

Venison Salad

TIME TO ALLOW: 10 minutes
SERVES 8

1 pound (450g) cold roast venison
2 ounces (50 g) gherkins
1 medium red capsicum
1 medium green capsicum
1 large onion
2 large tomatoes
1 clove garlic (crushed)
⅛ pint (75 ml) white vinegar
⅛ pint (75 ml) cold water
¼ pint (150 ml) soya oil
seasoning

Slice the venison and vegetables into thin strips, add garlic and seasoning, then add the vinegar and water. (By adding water the dressing is not too acidic, nor too oily.) Add the oil last and mix lightly. Taste and correct the seasoning.

This is an ideal way to use up leftover roast venison and makes an interesting side dish or an hors d'oeuvre in its own right.

Venison Cutlets with Oranges

TIME TO ALLOW: 30 minutes
SERVES 6

6 venison cutlets, each 8 to 9 ounces (200-250 g)
⅛ pint (75 ml) Grand Marnier
2 ounces (50 g) chopped shallots
2 ounces (50 g) butter
2 ounces (50 g) flour
¾ pint (450 ml) boiling venison stock (p.38)
pinch tarragon
pinch chopped parsley
seasoning
3 oranges, segmented
¾ pint (450 ml) orange juice
1 ounce (25 g) sugar

Marinate the cutlets overnight in the Grand Marnier.

Cook the shallots gently in butter for a minute or two. Remove from the heat, add the flour and cook for a few minutes, stirring occasionally. Remove from the heat again, add the boiling stock, herbs and seasoning and return to the heat. Bring slowly to the boil, and cook for a further 3-4 minutes, stirring all the time. Put this sauce to one side.

Drain and season the cutlets (reserving the marinade) and sauté for about 3-4 minutes on each side. Remove from the pan and keep warm on a serving dish.

Add the orange juice to the pan, then the sauce, and bring to the boil. Meanwhile, heat the orange segments gently in Grand Marnier and decorate the cutlets with them.

Add the sugar to the sauce, correct the seasoning, then strain the sauce over the decorated cutlets.

Venison Steaks with Green Peppercorn Sauce

TIME TO ALLOW: 15 to 20 minutes
SERVES 6

12 medallions cut from the filleted saddle each weighing about 3½ ounces (90 g)
1 ounce (25 g) mild prepared mustard

2 ounces (50 g) chopped shallots
2 ounces (50 g) butter
2 ounces (50 g) flour
½ pint (300 ml) boiling venison stock (p.38)
pinch tarragon
pinch chopped parsley
seasoning

1 medium onion, diced finely
1 fluid ounce (30 ml) brandy
¼ pint (150 ml) cream
1 ounce (25 g) drained green peppercorns

Cook the shallots in butter for a minute or two. Remove from the heat, add the flour and cook, stirring occasionally. Remove from the heat, add the boiling stock, the herbs and seasoning. Return to the heat, bring slowly to the boil and boil for 3-4 minutes, stirring all the time. Set aside.

Rub the steaks with mustard and seasoning. Pan fry on a high heat in a heavy bottomed pan for 3-4 minutes each side. Remove the steaks from the pan and place on a serving dish.

Add the finely diced onion to the pan and sauté for 2-3 minutes. Add the brandy and flame, then add the cream and green peppercorns and, lastly, the hot sauce. Bring to the boil and taste to correct the seasoning.

Spoon the sauce over the steaks and serve.

Venison Steaks with Cornichon Sauce

TIME TO ALLOW: 15 to 20 minutes
SERVES 6

12 medallions cut from the filleted saddle, each weighing about 3½ ounces (90 g)
1 ounce (25 g) prepared mild mustard

2 ounces (50 g) chopped shallots
2 ounces (50 g) butter
2 ounces (50 g) flour
½ pint (300 ml) boiling venison stock (p.38)
pinch tarragon
pinch chopped parsley
seasoning

⅛ pint (75 ml) white vinegar
¼ pint (150 ml) red wine
¼ pint (150 ml) water
juice from half a lemon
1 medium onion, chopped
1 small carrot, chopped
1 small stick celery, chopped
1 bay leaf

2 ounces (50 g) sharp pickled cornichons, thinly sliced

Cook the shallots in butter for a minute or two. Remove from the heat, add the flour and cook, stirring occasionally. Remove from the heat, add the stock, the herbs and seasoning and return to the heat. Bring slowly to the boil and boil for 3-4 minutes, stirring all the time. Set aside.

Place the vinegar, wine, water and vegetables in another saucepan. Bring to the boil and simmer until the mixture has reduced in volume by half. Strain into the basic sauce and add the cornichons.

Rub the steak with mustard and seasoning. Pan-fry on a high heat in a heavy-bottomed frying pan for 3-4 minutes on each side. Remove the steaks from the pan and place on a serving dish.

Spoon the hot sauce over the steaks to serve.

Roast Saddle of Venison

Any roast of venison can be served cold, but for best results the saddle should be used. For larger groups such as a party where a supper or buffet is served, the saddle can be roasted on the bone (in a piece suitable both for the number of people and the oven size), chilled, carved and replaced on the bone, making an attractive presentation.

TIME TO ALLOW: 12-15 minutes per pound (450 g)

saddle of venison
salt
freshly ground black pepper
oil

Prepare the piece of saddle by trimming carefully, then rub with salt and freshly ground black pepper and a little oil. Roast in a moderate oven (375°F/190°C/gas regulo 4-5).

For both hot or cold presentations, venison is better slightly underdone and pink throughout.

Roast Venison with Pâté de Foie

This dish makes an interesting and easily prepared cold starter for a meal and is also suitable for a supper.

TIME TO ALLOW: 15 minutes
SERVES 6

1 pound (450 g) cold roast venison, boned
8 ounces (200 g) prepared pâté de foie
¼ pint (150 ml) prepared mayonnaise
1 stem fresh tarragon

Slice the venison thinly (about 12-14 slices), spread with the pâté, roll up and dress on a serving dish. Chop the tarragon and mix with the mayonnaise to serve separately.

Roast Leg of Venison

TIME TO ALLOW: 3 hours
SERVES 6 to 8

half a leg venison, about 4 pounds (2 kg)
3 ounces (75 g) fatty bacon
3 ounces (75 g) flour
1 pint (600 ml) hot stock (venison, p.38, or vegetable)
¼ pint (150 ml) red wine
2 ounces (50 g) sour cream

Place the meat in an oven tray and cover with the bacon rashers. Brown in a hot oven (400-450°F/200-220°C/gas regulo 6-7), then cover the tray with foil and roast for 2-2½ hours in a moderate oven (375°F/190°C/gas regulo 4-5).

When the meat is tender and slightly pink throughout, remove from the tray and keep warm on a serving dish.

Mix the flour into the roasting tray fats until an even paste is formed and cook for 1-2 minutes. Remove from the heat and gradually stir in the hot stock, taking care to prevent lumps. Bring slowly to the boil, add the wine and simmer for a few minutes before adding the sour cream. Taste and correct the seasoning if required. The gravy should be a light brown in colour.

Roast Rack of Venison

TIME TO ALLOW: 1½ hours
SERVES 6 to 8

1 rack venison, about 6 pounds (3 kg)
seasoning
oil

Trim the rack of venison (cut from the saddle) and remove the fat so as to expose the rib bones. Clean around the bones and then season and rub with oil. Roast in a hot oven (425°F/220°C/gas regulo 7) for 30-45 minutes, until pink throughout. Carve and serve.

Venison Stew

TIME TO ALLOW: 2½ hours
SERVES 6

3 pounds (1.5 kg) boned venison (shoulder, neck or breast)
2 ounces (50 g) flour
8 ounces (200 g) tomatoes, chopped
3 medium onions, diced
2 cloves garlic, crushed
1 bay leaf
6 juniper berries, crushed and chopped
½ pint (300 ml) stock or water
seasoning
oil for frying

Dice the meat into bite-size pieces and dust with flour. Fry the onions and garlic in oil in a heavy-bottomed saucepan, then add the venison and continue to cook until the meat and onions are browned. Add the tomatoes, bay leaf, juniper berries, and just enough stock to cover the meat. Season and bring to the boil, then cover and simmer for 1½-2 hours, or until tender. Taste to correct the seasoning and serve.

Venison Casserole with Sour Cherries

TIME TO ALLOW: 2 hours (after marinating)
SERVES 6

3 pounds (1.5 kg) boned venison (shoulder, neck or breast)
¼ pint (150 ml) red wine
2 ounces (50 g) flour
1 ounce (25 g) tomato paste
¼ pint (150 ml) peanut oil
1 medium onion, diced
1 pound (450 g) pitted morello cherries
⅛ pint (75 ml) Kirsch
½ pint (300 ml) stock
oil

Dice the meat into bite-sized pieces and marinate in wine for 3-4 hours. Dry the meat, then flour and brown it in very hot oil. Add the seasoning, diced onion and tomato paste and enough stock to just cover the meat. Stir well and braise slowly in a warm oven (325°F/165°C/gas regulo 3) until tender (about 1½-2 hours).

Add the cherries and Kirsch, correct the seasoning and place in a clean serving casserole to serve.

Braised Venison in Red Wine

TIME TO ALLOW: 2½ hours
SERVES 6

3 pounds (1.5 kg) boned venison
2 ounces (50 g) flour
4 medium onions, diced finely
1 pint (600 ml) red wine
1 bay leaf
1 clove garlic, peeled
6 black peppercorns, cracked
seasoning
pinch of sugar
oil for frying

Cut the meat into neat slices about ½ inch (1 cm) thick and dust with flour. Heat the oil in a heavy-bottomed frying pan and brown the venison on both sides. Remove to a braising dish, add the remaining ingredients and season. Cover the dish and braise in a moderate oven (375°F/190°C/gas regulo 4-5) for 1½-2 hours, or until tender.

Venison Meatloaf

TIME TO ALLOW: 2 hours
SERVES 8

1 pound (450 g) venison fillet in one piece
2 pounds (1 kg) lean venison mince
3 eggs
seasoning
1 red capsicum, chopped
2 medium onions, chopped
1 pound (450 g) white breadcrumbs
⅛ pint (75 ml) cold water

Mix together lightly all the ingredients except the fillet, and season. A little extra cold water may be added if the mixture is too dry.

Choose a baking dish similar in size to a loaf of bread, grease, then dust with flour. Line the dish with half the mixture, place the fillet in the centre, then add the balance of the mixture around it. Cover with foil and bake in a moderate oven (375°F/190°C/gas regulo 5) for 1-1½ hours. The fillet should still be pink throughout.

Turn on to a serving dish, slice, and serve with redcurrant jelly.

Venison Soufflé

This is an ideal way to use up left-over venison roast.

TIME TO ALLOW: 20 minutes
SERVES 4

2 ounces (50 g) chopped shallots
2 ounces (50 g) butter
2 ounces (50 g) flour
½ pint (300 ml) boiling venison stock (p.38)
pinch tarragon
pinch chopped parsley
seasoning

6 ounces (150 g) minced, cooked venison
4 egg yolks
5 egg whites
pinch of salt
fine breadcrumbs

Cook the shallots in butter for a minute or two, remove from the heat, add the flour and cook for a few minutes, stirring occasionally. Remove from the heat again, add the boiling stock, the herbs and the seasoning. Return to the heat, bring slowly to the boil and boil for 3-4 minutes, stirring all the time.

Remove the sauce from the heat and cool slightly. Add the egg yolks one by one, then the minced venison. Beat the egg whites until they are stiff and fold lightly into the venison mixture.

Dust two soufflé dishes lightly with fine white breadcrumbs and half-fill each with the mixture. Bake in a moderately hot oven (375°F/190°C/gas regulo 5) for about 35 minutes.

HARE

HUNTING SEASON
Any time, but with specific local limitations.

The dark flesh of hare has a strong and interesting flavour which is set off to perfection in the traditional jugged hare. Older hares need to be braised or stewed because their flesh tends to be stringy, but young hares, distinguished by slender paws and claws hidden in fur, and ears which tear easily, are tender and suitable for roasting.

Hare can be eaten fresh, but hanging by the hind legs for 7-10 days before cleaning gives a better taste and makes it more digestible. A small bowl is placed underneath the head to catch the blood which should have a drop of vinegar added to stop it coagulating.

Skinning a hare is relatively easy since the skin is loosely attached. Start at the hind legs and slit down the inside of each thigh, then along the belly and then remove the skin in one piece. Save the blood, which collects in the diaphragm while hanging, for thickening casseroles, and reserve the liver, kidneys, heart and well-trimmed lungs.

Prime cuts are the hind legs and the saddle (the back) which can be cut into two or three pieces. The shoulders or forequarters are tender on young hare but very bony and are usually used to make stock.

Hare Stock

TIME TO ALLOW: 2 hours

2 pounds (1 kg) raw bones (saddle, legs and whole shoulders)
2 pints (1200 ml) water
8 ounces (200 g) vegetables (carrot, onion, celery, etc)
1 bay leaf
6 peppercorns

Cover the stock bones with cold water and bring to the boil. Add the vegetables, bay leaf and peppercorns and simmer for an hour. Remove the shoulders, take the meat off the bone and set aside for soup recipes. Return the bones to the stock for a further 1 hour's simmering then strain.

Hare Soup

TIME TO ALLOW: 30 minutes (from prepared stock)
SERVES 6

2 pints (1200 ml) hot hare stock (above)
2 ounces (50 g) butter
1 medium onion, chopped finely
1 clove garlic, crushed
2 ounces (50 g) flour
1 ounce (25 g) tomato paste

Melt the butter in a saucepan and fry the onion and garlic gently until they are a golden colour. Stir in the flour and continue to cook on a low heat until light brown. Add the tomato paste and cook for a few minutes. Remove from heat and add the hot stock gradually, stirring all the time to avoid lumps. Bring to the boil and season to taste.

Dice the shoulder meat reserved from stock-making and add to the soup. Return to the boil.

It is traditional to serve a glass of port with hare soup.

Hare and Peanut Broth

TIME TO ALLOW: 30 minutes (from prepared stock)
SERVES 8

2 pints (1200 ml) hare stock (opposite)
1 medium onion, chopped
1 clove garlic, crushed
1 green capsicum, chopped
1 red capsicum, chopped
1 teaspoon curry powder (or a generous pinch each of chilli, saffron,
    turmeric, coriander)
oil for frying
2 ounces (50 g) crunchy peanut butter
1 clove, chopped finely
1 bay leaf
2 ounces (50 g) soya sauce
⅛ pint (75 ml) coconut cream

OPTIONAL
1 tablespoon chilli sauce

Sauté the onion, garlic, peppers and curry powder gently for 3-4 minutes, then add the crunchy peanut butter and other ingredients. Mix to an even paste and then add the stock, blending thoroughly.

Bring to the boil, season to taste and simmer until all the ingredients are tender (about 10 minutes). Add the hare meat reserved from stock-making and return to the boil then serve.

This is a spicy soup and if you enjoy such flavours the addition of chilli sauce will enhance it even further.

Roast Hare

By roasting the hare whole, the saddle and hind legs can be served (four portions) and the bones retained for stock to make soups and sauces. The meat from the shoulders can be used as a garnish for soups.

TIME TO ALLOW: 1 hour
SERVES 4

1 hare, about 5 pounds (2.5 kg)
3 ounces (75 g) flour
1 pint (600 ml) hot stock (hare, p.52 or vegetable)
¼ pint (150 ml) red wine

Place the hare in a roasting tray rib-side down, with the legs open to ensure even cooking. Rub with salt, pepper and oil, cover with foil and roast in a moderate oven (375°F/190°C/gas regulo 4-5) for approximately 45 minutes. It is quite acceptable to serve hare slightly pink. When done, remove from the roasting tray and keep warm.

Add the flour to the pan juices, mix to an even paste and cook for 1-2 minutes. Remove from the heat and add the stock gradually. Stir until boiling and simmer for a few minutes, season, then add the red wine. Return to the boil, strain and serve.

Meanwhile, joint the hare into serving portions by removing the two hind legs and running a knife down the backbone to remove the saddle from each side of the spine.

Roast Hare with Apple and Cranberry Sauce

TIME TO ALLOW: 1 hour
SERVES 4

1 hare, about 5 pounds (2.5 kg)
3 ounces (75 g) flour
1 pint (600 ml) hot stock (hare, p.52 or vegetable)
¼ pint (150 ml) ruby port
2 crisp apples
3 ounces (75 g) fresh cranberries

Prepare and roast the hare as in the basic roast hare recipe (opposite), but when making the sauce add port in place of the red wine. Return the sauce to the boil, simmer for a few minutes and then strain into a clean saucepan.

Peel the apples and slice neatly, and wash the cranberries. Add to the sauce, bring gently to the boil and correct the seasoning. If the sauce is too sour, a pinch of sugar will rectify this.

Braised Legs of Hare with Herb Stuffing

TIME TO ALLOW: 1¼ hours
SERVES 4

4 legs of hare, each about 9 ounces (225 g)
1 small onion, chopped
1 clove garlic, crushed
oil for frying
6 ounces (150 g) sliced white bread, diced
⅛ pint (75 ml) milk
3 ounces (75 g) chopped fresh herbs — parsley, basil, rosemary,
   thyme (or 1 ounce (25 g) dried mixed herbs)
1 egg
¾ pint (450 ml) hare stock (p.52), or water
¼ pint (150 ml) red wine
seasoning
flour

To prepare the stuffing: pan-fry the onion and garlic lightly in a little oil.
Remove from the heat and add the diced bread. Season and add the milk,
herbs and egg. Mix thoroughly.

To prepare the legs: Remove the bone from the legs, making an incision
on the inside thigh. Take care not to pierce the other side of the leg. Divide
the stuffing into 4 equal parts and place inside the legs, securing with a
toothpick. Dust the legs with seasoned flour.

Pre-heat a deep casserole dish in a hot oven (425°F/220°C/gas regulo
7). Oil the dish and arrange the hare legs in it. Return to the oven for 10
minutes, then turn the legs and add the stock and red wine and a little
seasoning. Cover the dish with a lid or foil and reduce the oven temperature
to 375°F/190°C/gas regulo 4-5. Braise until tender, about 45 minutes.

Spoon the sauce over the legs and serve.

Saddle of Hare with Beetroot and Lime

TIME TO ALLOW: 30 to 40 minutes
SERVES 4

2 saddles of hare, each about 1½ pounds (650 g)
3 fresh limes
2 ounces (50 g) chopped shallots
2 ounces (50 g) butter
2 ounces (50 g) flour
1 pint (600 ml) hare stock (p.52) or water
4 ounces (100 g) cooked beetroot cut into thin strips
pinch sugar
seasoning

Grate the zest of the limes finely and set aside. Squeeze the limes and pour the juice over the hare saddles and leave for two hours, turning occasionally so that they are evenly marinated.

Drain the saddles (reserving the marinade), dry them with kitchen paper and rub with a little oil and seasoning. Roast in a hot oven (425°F/220°C/gas regulo 7) for 20 minutes.

Meanwhile prepare the sauce. Sauté the shallots in butter for 1-2 minutes and remove from the heat. Stir in the flour and then cook until light brown in colour. Remove from the heat again, gradually add the hot stock and bring to the boil, stirring continuously. Simmer for a few minutes and then add the lime zest and beetroot and half of the lime juice marinade. Return to the boil then set aside.

When the hare is done remove to a serving tray and keep warm.

Add the balance of the lime juice marinade to the roasting tray with a touch of water. Bring to the boil and add a pinch of sugar, then strain into the beetroot sauce. Bring the sauce to the boil again and correct the seasoning.

Serve sauce separately.

Saddle of Hare with Vinegar and Cream

TIME TO ALLOW: 30 minutes
SERVES 4

2 saddles, each about 1½ pounds (650 g)
3 ounces (75 g) fatty bacon
½ pint (300 ml) white wine
⅛ pint (75 ml) white vinegar
½ pint (300 ml) cream
2 spring onions
oil
seasoning

Season the saddles, rub with oil and cover with bacon. Roast in a hot oven (425°F/220°C/gas regulo 7) for 20 minutes (keeping the meat underdone). Remove saddles and place them on a serving tray and keep warm.

Add the wine and vinegar to the roasting tray and cook until reduced in volume by half. Add the cream and cook until the sauce has the consistency of lightly whipped cream. Taste to correct the seasoning, add the finely sliced spring onions and pour some of the sauce over the saddles. Serve the remainder of the sauce separately.

Hare Casserole with Mushrooms and Tomatoes

This dish is suitable for an older hare which would not make good roasting.

TIME TO ALLOW: 1½-2 hours
SERVES 4-6

1 hare, 4-5 pounds (2-2.5 kg)
2 onions
oil for frying
½ pint (300 ml) stock or water
½ pint (300 ml) red wine
flour
8 ounces (200 g) firm ripe tomatoes
8 ounces (200 g) button mushrooms
2 cloves garlic

Reserve the heart, liver, kidneys and blood separately. Portion the hare into two shoulders, two legs and the saddle (divided into two), trimming carefully. Place all the trimmings and one chopped onion in a saucepan, fry gently, then cover with stock. Bring to the boil and skim, then simmer for approximately 30 minutes.

Flour the offal and fry lightly, add the wine and simmer for 5 minutes. Set aside to cool.

Place the hare portions in the casserole with the other chopped onion and the garlic, fry together for a few minutes, then strain the stock into it to about two-thirds full. Place the casserole in a moderate oven (375°F/190°C/gas regulo 5) and cook until nearly tender (about 1 hour).

Remove the offal from the wine, chop finely and return to the saucepan together with the blood.

About 10 minutes before serving, add the washed mushrooms and diced, peeled tomatoes to the casserole. Lastly add the offal, blood and wine mixture. Allow to thicken (but not to boil) and serve.

VARIATION

For a change try hare casserole with chestnut sauce. Instead of adding mushrooms and tomatoes as above, stir in an 8 ounce (200 g) can of chesnut purée.

Jugged Hare

Traditionally prepared jugged hare can only be made with the whole hare, as the blood is reserved to thicken the sauce.

TIME TO ALLOW: 6 hours for preparation and marinating
2 hours for cooking
SERVES 4 to 6

MARINADE
½ pint (300 ml) red wine
⅛ pint (75 ml) white vinegar
1 pound (450 g) washed, peeled and sliced vegetables (carrot, onion, celery)
2 bay leaves
6 juniper berries
10 peppercorns
2 cloves garlic
¼ pint (150 ml) oil

1 young hare, about 5 pounds (2.5 kg)
2 ounces (50 g) butter
2 cloves garlic, crushed
1 pint (600 ml) stock or water
½ pint (300 ml) red wine
1 ounce (25 g) flour
1 tablespoon (25 g) tomato paste
seasoning

Carefully skin the hare and make an incision along the belly. Remove the intestines, heart, liver, etc., reserving the blood in a bowl. Joint the hare into 2 legs, 2 shoulders and a saddle, divided in two.

Mix all the ingredients for the marinade and marinate the hare portions for 5-6 hours, turning frequently.

Drain or pat dry the joints. Melt the butter in a large heavy-bottomed frying pan and brown the hare pieces evenly on all sides. Season and remove the hare pieces from the pan and keep warm.

Mix the flour in with the butter, then the tomato paste and the marinade, stirring thoroughly. Replace the hare in the frying pan, bring to the boil, then skim and add the garlic, stock and wine.

Cover and simmer until the hare is tender, about 30-45 minutes. Remove the hare to a serving dish and keep warm.

Return the sauce to the boil and taste to correct the seasoning. Thicken by gradually adding the blood. After adding the blood the sauce must not boil. Strain the sauce and pour over the hare.

GARNISH
4 ounces (100 g) button mushrooms, washed
4 ounces (100 g) button onions, peeled
4 ounces (100 g) bacon rashers cut into small strips
4 ounces (100 g) bread
1 ounce (25 g) butter
Seasoning

Melt the butter in a heavy-bottomed frying pan and gently brown the onions. Season, then remove from the pan. Brown the mushrooms, season, and remove from the pan.

Cut the bacon into 2½ inch (6 cm) strips and brown, then remove from the pan. Cut the bread into heart-shaped pieces and fry until golden.

Mix the garnish with the jugged hare and arrange the heart-shaped croutons with the points just in the sauce. Sprinkle with chopped parsley.

Mixed Hare Salad with Yoghurt Dressing

TIME TO ALLOW: 15 minutes (with cooked meat)
SERVES 4 entrées

1 saddle of hare, roasted and chilled
1 orange, segmented, and juice
8 button mushrooms, washed and cut in half
2 gherkins, sliced thinly
1 bunch washed watercress (about a handful)
½ pint (300 ml) plain yoghurt

Roast the saddle ahead of time, so that it is well chilled before using in the salad. (Rub with a little oil and seasoning and roast in a hot oven (425°F/220°C/gas regulo 7) for 20 minutes.)

Bone the saddle and slice on an angle across the grain. Mix with the other ingredients, except the yoghurt, and season to taste. Lastly add the yoghurt, mixing lightly. Dress on lettuce on entrée plates.

Cold Saddle of Hare with Red Cabbage Salad

TIME TO ALLOW: 15 minutes (with cooked meat)
SERVES 4 entrées

1 saddle of hare, roasted and chilled (see opposite)
½ red cabbage
1 small onion
1 apple
⅛ pint (75 ml) white vinegar
⅛ pint (75 ml) cold water
pinch of sugar
seasoning
¼ pint (150 ml) soya oil

Shred the cabbage and onion finely. Peel and core the apple and cut into thin strips. Mix with the cabbage, then add the vinegar, water, seasoning and sugar, and lastly, the oil.

Bone the saddle and slice on an angle across the grain.

Divide the red cabbage salad into four and dress on to four entrée plates. Garnish with the hare slices, about 3-4 per serving.

A suitable sauce to accompany this would be:

⅛ pint (75 ml) prepared mayonnaise
1 tablespoon grain mustard
juice of 1 lemon

Mix all ingredients and serve.

Hare Liver Pâté

If you have had a particularly successful hunting expedition reserve all the hare livers and prepare this simple pâté.

TIME TO ALLOW: 20 to 30 minutes, plus 30 minutes for cooling
SUFFICIENT FOR 8 entrée pots

1 pound (450g) hare livers
2 ounces (50 g) butter
2 medium onions, sliced
4 ounces (100 g) streaky bacon
1 clove garlic, crushed
1 bay leaf
1 small sprig each of thyme, rosemary and marjoram
pinch allspice
1/8 pint (75 ml) brandy
1/2 pint (300 ml) cream

Melt the butter in a heavy-bottomed pan and sauté the onions. When nearly tender add the bacon, garlic and livers, then the herbs. Cook thoroughly over a low heat, seasoning to taste.

Remove the bay leaf and the other fresh herbs then flame with brandy. Mince or blend the mixture, gradually adding the cream.

While still warm spoon into serving dishes and refrigerate.

See photograph opposite p.40

RABBIT

HUNTING SEASON
Any time

The rabbit is smaller than a hare with a shorter head and ears and smaller hind legs and feet. Wild rabbit has dark, firm gamey-flavoured flesh.

Unlike hare, rabbit is raised commercially for meat and its pelt. The domestic or commercially bred rabbit is larger than the wild species and should be eaten relatively young — about three to four months. Its flesh will be paler with a more delicate taste and it responds to a well-flavoured marinade or stuffing.

Wild rabbit is gutted as soon as it is killed and hung by its hind legs for twenty-four hours. It is skinned and jointed in the same way as hare. Some people find the flesh of wild rabbit difficult to digest; it can be improved by soaking in a marinade of water and vinegar (1 teaspoon vinegar to 1 pint water) for 12 hours before cooking.

Rabbit Stock

TIME TO ALLOW: 2 hours

2 pounds (1 kg) raw bones (saddle, shoulders)
2 pints (1200 ml) water
8 ounces (200 g) vegetables (carrot, onion, celery, etc.)
1 bay leaf
6 peppercorns

Cover the bones with cold water and bring to the boil. Add the vegetables, bay leaf and peppercorns and simmer for an hour. Remove the shoulders, take the meat off the bone and set aside for soup. Return the bones to the stock for a further 1 hour's simmering then strain.

Chilled Rabbit and Raspberry Soup

TIME TO ALLOW: 30 minutes from prepared stock, plus cooling time
SERVES 6

2 pints (1200 ml) rabbit stock
1½ ounces (35 g) butter
1½ ounces (35 g) flour
8 ounces (200 g) fresh or frozen raspberries
seasoning
pinch of sugar
white vinegar

Melt the butter in a saucepan, then add the flour and cook for a few minutes on a low heat without allowing colouring. Cool slightly, then add the hot stock, stirring constantly to avoid lumps. Bring to the boil and season to taste. Add the raspberries and a touch of white vinegar, which gives a beautiful piquant flavour. Allow to cool, then mix thoroughly in a blender. Taste the soup when it is cold because chilled dishes require a little more seasoning to ensure they are not insipid. Chill to serve.

Rabbit and Spinach Soup

TIME TO ALLOW: 30 minutes (from prepared stock)
SERVES 6

2 pints (1200 ml) hot rabbit stock (opposite)
2 ounces (50 g) butter
2 ounces (50 g) flour
6 ounces (150 g) washed spinach
1/8 pint (75 ml) cream

Melt the butter in a saucepan then add the flour, cook for a few minutes on a low heat without colouring, and allow to cool slightly. Add the hot stock, stirring constantly to avoid lumps. Bring to the boil and season to taste.

Plunge the washed spinach into boiling water and return to the boil. As soon as it has reboiled, remove from heat and run the spinach under cold water to prevent further cooking. Squeeze as much water as possible from the spinach and cut into thin strips.

Cut the rabbit reserved from the stock into thin strips and add the spinach and rabbit to the soup. Lastly add the cream, and serve.

Casserole of Rabbit

TIME TO ALLOW: 45 minutes
SERVES 4

1 rabbit, about 5 pounds (2.5 kg)
1 medium onion, chopped
4 ounces (100 g) chopped bacon rashers
4 ounces (100 g) mixed green and black olives
1 clove garlic, crushed
1 ounce (25 g) chopped herbs (rosemary, parsley and thyme)
½ pint (300 ml) white wine
flour
oil
seasoning

Cut the rabbit into joints, dust with flour, season, and sauté in moderately hot oil, browning on all sides, then place in a casserole.

Fry the onion and bacon in the pan, add the garlic and fry a little longer. Add the wine and herbs. Pour this mixture into the casserole. Bake in a moderate oven (375°F/190°C/gas regulo 4-5) for 15-20 minutes or until tender. Season to taste.

Rabbit Sauté with Frankfurters

TIME TO ALLOW: 30 minutes
SERVES 4

1 rabbit, about 5 pounds (2.5 kg)
1 medium onion, sliced thinly
1 ounce (25 g) French mustard
½ pint (300 ml) white wine
8 ounces (200 g) frankfurters, sliced on an angle
flour
oil
seasoning

Cut the rabbit into joints (two shoulders, two legs, saddle cut into two), and flour the pieces.

Heat a heavy-bottomed frying pan and fry the onions lightly. Add the rabbit and season. Turn the rabbit to brown evenly and when nearly tender (about 15 minutes) add the mustard. Stir thoroughly, then add the wine and cook for a few minutes.

Just before serving add the frankfurters and return to the boil to heat them through. Serve.

Rabbit Sauté with Pimento Sauce

TIME TO ALLOW: 30 minutes
SERVES 4

1 rabbit, about 5 pounds (2.5 kg)
2 large sweet red pimento cut into thin strips
1 medium green pimento cut into thin strips
1 clove garlic, crushed
½ pint (300 ml) white wine
flour
oil
seasoning

Cut the rabbit into joints (two shoulders, two legs, saddle cut into two).
Heat a heavy-bottomed frying pan, flour the joints and sauté, browning
lightly on both sides. Season to taste. When nearly cooked through (about
15 minutes) remove from the pan and keep warm.

Place the pimento and garlic into the pan and fry gently, add the white
wine and bring to the boil. Simmer until the mixture has reduced by a third,
then return the rabbit to the pan and bring to the boil. Taste to correct
the seasoning of the sauce and serve.

Braised Rabbit with Horseradish and Port

TIME TO ALLOW: 30 minutes
SERVES 4

1 rabbit, about 5 pounds (2.5 kg)
1 medium onion, chopped finely
1 clove garlic, crushed
4 ounces (100 g) scraped horseradish
¼ pint (150 ml) port
½ pint (300 ml) stock or water
flour
oil
seasoning

Remove the front legs from the rabbit and reserve for stock. Place rabbit rib-side down with the legs open, season and dust with flour. Brown in hot oil in a deep dish. (An electric frying pan with a close-fitting lid would be suitable.) Add the onions and garlic, brown further, and season. Add the port and simmer until it has been reduced by a third, then add the stock.

Cover the dish and cook in a moderate oven (375°F/190°C/gas regulo 4-5). This temperature is also suitable for electric frying pan cooking. When tender, approximately 20 minutes, add the horseradish and cook for a few minutes longer.

Rabbit with Celery and Carrots

TIME TO ALLOW: 45 minutes
SERVES 4

1 rabbit, about 5 pounds (2.5 kg)
3 fresh basil leaves
4 ounces (100 g) celery cut into matchstick-sized strips
4 ounces (100 g) carrots cut into matchstick-sized strips
1 bay leaf
oil
flour
seasoning

Remove the front legs from the rabbit and reserve for stock. Place the rabbit rib-side down with the legs open, season and dust with flour. Brown the pieces in hot oil in a deep dish or an electric frying pan. Cook until the rabbit is nearly tender, about 15 minutes, then add the herbs, celery, and carrots. Continue to cook for a further 5-10 minutes, or until tender.

Crumbed Rabbit Legs with Lemon

TIME TO ALLOW: 45 minutes
SERVES 4

4 hind legs of rabbit, each about 6-8 ounces (150-200 g)
1 egg
¼ pint (150 ml) milk
flour
breadcrumbs
seasoning
1 lemon, cut into wedges
oil for frying

Trim the rabbit legs and carefully remove the thigh bone by making an incision along the bone on the inside of the leg. Beat the egg and mix in the milk. Season the flour, pass the rabbit legs through the flour, shaking off any excess, then dip into the egg-wash, and then in the breadcrumbs, patting to ensure an even coating.

Heat the oil in a heavy-bottomed frying pan and brown the crumbed legs evenly, turning down the heat slightly to cook the rabbit through once browned. Cook for 15-20 minutes, or until tender.

Drain the legs on kitchen paper and place on a serving dish. Decorate with lemon wedges and a sprig of fresh dill or fennel.

Rabbit Fillets in Pastry

TIME TO ALLOW: 45 minutes
SERVES 8 snack portions

2 saddles of rabbit, each about 1½ pounds (650 g)
1 pound (450 g) puff pastry
egg wash

Roast the saddles in a hot oven (425°F/220°C/gas regulo 7) for 20-25 minutes, or until just cooked. Allow to cool then remove the fillets from the bone.

Roll the pastry to ⅛ inch (3 mm) thick and place the fillets on the pastry so that they will be completely surrounded by pastry when rolled up (as in sausage rolls). Brush with the egg wash and cut into 2 inch (50 mm) lengths.

Bake in a moderate oven (375°F/190°C/gas regulo 4-5) for 20-25 minutes, or until cooked.

Chilled Rabbit Fillets with Vinaigrette

TIME TO ALLOW: 45 minutes, plus cooling time
SERVES 4

2 saddles of rabbit, each about 1½ pounds (650 g)
¼ pint (150 ml) white vinegar
½ pint (300 ml) oil
⅛ pint (75 ml) water
2 hard-boiled eggs, chopped finely
2 sprigs of parsley, chopped finely
oil
seasoning
freshly ground black pepper
1 clove crushed garlic (optional)

Roast the saddles in a hot oven (425°F/220°C/gas regulo 7) for 20-25 minutes, or until just cooked. Allow to cool then remove the fillets from the bone, slice them across the grain and dress on lettuce.

Blend all the other ingredients and serve separately.

Rabbit and Mushroom Salad

TIME TO ALLOW: 45 minutes, plus cooling time
SERVES 4

2 saddles of rabbit, each about 1½ pounds (650 g)
8 ounces (200 g) button mushrooms, washed and halved
¼ pint (150 ml) prepared mayonnaise
½ pint (300 ml) sour cream
juice of 1 lemon
1 ounce (25 g) chopped chives

Roast the saddles in a hot oven (425°F/220°C/gas regulo 7) for 20-25 minutes, or until just cooked. Allow to cool and remove the fillets from the bone. Slice across the grain and season.

Blend with all the other ingredients and serve.

WILD BOAR

Wild boar have been extinct in Britain since the seventeenth century, although their breeding for the table is now being considered. Wild boar pâté and similar delicacies are imported from Europe and appear on our supermarket shelves but our nearest access to wild boar for the sportsman is Holland and France. In France the general term for it is *sanglier*, but the names for it alter according to the animal's age. Up to six months, wild boar is known as *marcassin*; from six months to a year it is *bête rousse*; from one to two years, *bête de compagnie*; at two years it becomes *ragot*; at three, *sanglier à son tiers ans* and, at four, *à quartenier*. Thereafter it is *porc entier*.

The flesh of the wild boar is lean, dark and has a pronounced gamey taste. All the recipes in this section can be used for the same cuts of pork.

Wild Pork Stock

TIME TO ALLOW: 4 hours

2 pounds (1 kg) raw pork bones
2 pints (1200 ml) water
8 ounces (200 g) vegetables (carrot, onion, celery, leek)
1 bay leaf
6 peppercorns

Brown the chopped pork bones in a hot oven with the vegetables. Place the bones in a saucepan, cover with cold water and bring to the boil. If the scum is dirty, discard the water, wash the bones and re-cover with cold water. Return to the boil, add the other ingredients and simmer gently for 3-4 hours. It may be necessary to top up the stock with cold water during the simmering. Skim the stock and then strain.

Wild Pork and Apple Soup

TIME TO ALLOW: 40 minutes, using prepared stock
SERVES 6

2 pints (1200 ml) wild pork stock
2 ounces (50 g) butter
2 ounces (50 g) flour
8 ounces (200 g) sour cooking apples, peeled and cored
pinch of sugar
juice of ½ lemon
seasoning

Melt the butter in a saucepan then add the flour and cook slowly until brown in colour. Remove from the heat and add the hot stock gradually, stirring briskly to avoid lumps. Bring to the boil, add seasoning and lemon juice, then simmer for 30 minutes.

Cut the apples into wedges and add to the soup. Cook for a further 10 minutes.

A little Calvados (apple liqueur) added to the soup enhances the flavour.

Wild Pork and Vegetable Broth

TIME TO ALLOW: 1½ hours, using prepared stock
SERVES 6

2 pints (1200 ml) wild pork stock
1 ounce (25 g) barley
12 ounces (300 g) vegetables (carrot, onion, celery, leek)
bay leaf
seasoning

Prepare the stock as in the recipe opposite but do not brown the bones.
   Wash the barley, then add to the stock and simmer for approximately
1 hour. Peel and dice the vegetables and add to the soup along with the
bay leaf and seasoning. Bring the soup to the boil and simmer for 30 minutes,
or until the vegetables are tender.
   Taste and correct seasoning if necessary.

Wild Pork Loin Roasted with Spinach

TIME TO ALLOW: 2 hours
SERVES 6

1 loin of wild pork, boned and trimmed, about 3 pounds (1.5 kg)
1 pound (450 g) spinach, washed and blanched in boiling water
oil
seasoning
1 clove crushed garlic

Lay the loin down flat and spread with the spinach and garlic. Season, then
roll the fillet and secure with string. Roast in a moderate oven
(375°F/190°C/gas regulo 4-5) for 1-1½ hours, or until tender. Slice and
serve.
   A plain roast gravy would be a suitable accompaniment.

Roast Wild Pork with Apple Sauce

TIME TO ALLOW: 5 hours
SERVES 20 (approximately)

1 leg wild pork, about 10-12 pounds (4-5 kg)
2 pints (1200 ml) stock or water
4 ounces (100 g) flour
4 ounces (100 g) butter
3 cloves garlic, crushed
seasoning
½ pint (300 ml) prepared apple sauce

Skin the pork and rub with oil and garlic. Season well and place in a roasting dish along with the stock. Cover with foil and roast in a moderate oven (375°F/190°C/gas regulo 4-5) for 3-4 hours, or until tender. Turn over halfway through cooking time, to ensure even cooking. Remove the pork from the tray and keep warm.

Melt the butter in a saucepan, then add the flour and cook on a low heat until slighty browned. Allow to cool, then strain in the hot stock from the roasting tray, stirring constantly. Season to taste and bring to the boil. If sauce becomes too thick due to evaporation of the roasting tray stock, add a little stock or water to correct the consistency. Taste to check the seasoning.

Carve the roast and serve the gravy and apple sauce separately.

This is equally delicious served cold for banquets, omitting the gravy and served with apple sauce.

Roast Leg of Wild Boar with Rose Petal Sauce

TIME TO ALLOW: 4½ hours
SERVES approximately 15 to 20

1 leg of wild boar, about 10 pounds (4.5 kg)
1 pint (600 ml) stock or water
2 ounces (50 g) flour
4 cloves garlic, crushed
2-3 drops rose oil (available from a chemist)
12 ounces (300 g) rose petal jelly
seasoning
pinch of sugar
oil

Rub the leg with salt, pepper, sugar and oil. Place in a roasting tray with a generous amount of water. Cover the dish with foil and roast in a moderate oven (375°F/190°C/gas regulo 4-5) for 3-4 hours, or until tender. Turn the meat after two hours to ensure even cooking.

Remove the meat from the tray and set aside until ready to serve. When the roasting tray juices are cool, add the flour and whisk thoroughly. Stir in the hot stock (or water) and rose oil. Bring to the boil and simmer for 10 minutes, then add the rose petal jelly and simmer for a further 5 minutes. Correct the seasoning and strain.

Carve the roast and serve the sauce separately.

Braised Wild Pork with Ginger and Black Beans

TIME TO ALLOW: 2½ hours
SERVES 4

2 pounds (1 kg) boned shoulder meat of boar, cubed
2 medium onions, chopped roughly
oil
flour
½ pint (300 ml) stock (or water)
¼ pint (150 ml) green ginger wine
2 ounces (50 g) finely chopped fresh ginger
2 ounces (50 g) finely chopped black beans
1 large red or green pepper, sliced
1 clove garlic, crushed
⅛ pint (75 ml) dry sherry

Fry onions until light brown in colour in a deep, heavy bottomed frying-pan. In a separate pan, heated to high heat, brown the lightly-floured pork in oil. When it is thoroughly browned on all sides, place it on top of the onions then add ginger wine and stock. Cover with a lid. Cook on low heat (350°F/175°C/gas regulo 3) until nearly tender, about 1½-2 hours.

Add the remaining ingredients and cook a further 10 minutes. If the sauce is too thin, rub a little butter into flour and whisk it in to thicken.

Boar Steaks on Sauerkraut

TIME TO ALLOW: 30 minutes
SERVES 6

12 boar steaks, each 4 ounces (100 g)
1 medium onion, chopped
2 rashers bacon, chopped
1 pound (450 g) sauerkraut
⅛ pint (75 ml) white vinegar
¼ pint (150 ml) white wine
pinch of sugar
2 juniper berries
pinch of caraway seeds
1 bay leaf
1 large raw potato, grated very finely
2 ounces (50 g) flour
1 pint (600 ml) hot stock or water
oil
seasoning

Sauté the onion in a little oil in a saucepan until transparent. Add the bacon and cook a little longer, then add the sauerkraut, vinegar and wine. Season with a pinch of sugar, caraway seeds, juniper berries and bay leaf. Bring to the boil, check the seasoning, then stir in the grated potato and return to the boil until the sauerkraut thickens. Remove from the heat and re-heat when required.

Heat a heavy-bottomed frying pan and sauté the steaks until done (about 15 minutes). Remove the steaks and add the flour to the pan. Cook for a few minutes then add the hot stock, stirring constantly. Bring to the boil and correct the seasoning.

Dress the steaks on the sauerkraut and coat with the sauce to serve.

Wild Pork Medallions with Orange Sauce

TIME TO ALLOW: 30 minutes
SERVES 6

6 loin steaks of wild boar, each 8 ounces (200 g)
4 ounces (100 g) sugar
½ pint (300 ml) stock or water
⅛ pint (75 ml) red wine
⅛ pint (75 ml) Grand Marnier or other orange liqueur
juice of 2 oranges
grated zest of 4 oranges
seasoning

ORANGE SAUCE
Melt the sugar in a saucepan on a low heat until caramelised. Add the rest
of the ingredients immediately and bring to the boil. Season lightly and
simmer for 30 minutes. This can be prepared in advance.

Sauté the boar steaks in a heavy-bottomed frying pan, browning on both
sides until done (10-15 minutes altogether). Season. De-glaze the frying pan
by adding a little water, then pour into the orange sauce.
   Ladle the sauce over the steaks and serve.

Chilled Roast Boar Fillet
with Curry and Mango Chutney

TIME TO ALLOW: 2 hours
SERVES 4, or 8 appetisers

2 pounds (1 kg) fillet of boar, trimmed and boned
3 cloves garlic, crushed
1 ounce (25 g) curry powder
2 cloves, crushed and chopped
oil
seasoning
prepared mango chutney

Rub the fillet with the curry, garlic, cloves and seasoning. Then rub with the oil. Allow to stand for 1 hour.

Roast in a moderate oven (375°F/190°C/gas regulo 4-5) until done, approximately 1-1¼ hours. Remove the meat from the tray and allow to cool.

Slice the meat thinly and serve with mango chutney.

This dish is suitable both as a cold appetiser or as a main course served with a salad.

Roast Fillet of Wild Boar with Apples and Prunes

TIME TO ALLOW: 2 hours
SERVES 4

2 pounds (1 kg) trimmed and boned fillet of boar
2 apples, peeled and cored, sliced into wedges
4 ounces (100 g) pitted prunes
1 pint (600 ml) hot stock (or water)
2 ounces (50 g) flour
1 clove garlic, crushed
pinch caraway seeds
seasoning
oil

With a sharp knife, make an incision through the centre of the fillet. Fill alternately with the apples and prunes. Rub the fillet with salt, freshly ground black pepper, caraway seeds, garlic and oil. Place in a roasting dish with a little water and roast in a moderate oven (375°F/190°C/gas regulo 4-5) until tender, approximately 1-1¼ hours. Remove and set aside.

Stir flour into the roasting tray residue, mixing to a smooth paste, and cook for a few minutes on the top element, before adding hot stock. Bring to the boil and correct the seasoning.

Carve onto a serving dish and coat with sauce.

GOAT

In this country the goat is a domesticated animal. During the last few years there has been a great interest in rearing goats, mainly because of the widespread use of goat's milk, which is considered to be beneficial for the treatment of some allergies, and a bigger market for various kinds of goat's cheese. Goat meat is widely used in Middle Eastern cooking, as well as in the cooking of other countries. It is available from specialist butchers.

Goat is best eaten young. The leg and saddle are suitable for roasting, the shoulder should be diced for braising and stewing. The flesh of an older animal can be rather tough and very strongly flavoured.

Goat and Fetta Salad

TIME TO ALLOW: 1½ hours
SERVES 4 luncheons, or 8 cold starters

2 pounds (1 kg) boned saddle of goat, roasted and served cold
8 ounces (200 g) fetta cheese
1 medium onion, shredded finely
2 medium tomatoes, cored and cut into wedges
1 ounce (25 g) shelled walnuts
⅛ pint (75 ml) white vinegar
⅛ pint (75 ml) cold water
¼ pint (150 ml) soya bean or olive oil
1/16 pint (35 ml) walnut oil
seasoning

Place the meat in a roasting tray and rub all over with oil. Roast in a moderately hot oven (400°F/205°C/gas regulo 6) for 30-45 minutes, or until tender. Remove from the tray and leave the meat to cool.

Bone, trim and slice the meat in thin slices across the grain on an angle.

Cut the fetta into oblong slices 2 inch x 1 inch (5 cm x 2.5 cm). Combine all the dry ingredients, season, then add the vinegar and water. Add the oils last and mix lightly. Taste to correct the seasoning.

Marinated Goat with Coconut Cream

TIME TO ALLOW: 2 hours, including cooling time
SERVES 6-8 entrées

1 shoulder of goat, about 3 pounds (1.5 kg)
2 medium onions, peeled and sliced
1 medium carrot, peeled and sliced
2 stalks celery, sliced
12 black peppercorns

1 medium onion, chopped finely
3 spring onions, sliced finely
6 chives, sliced finely
juice from 6 limes
16 ounces (500 g) tin of coconut cream or
    2 cups desiccated coconut
    2½ cups hot water
seasoning

In a large pot place the goat, onions, carrot, celery and peppercorns and salt. Top up with water and bring to the boil. Simmer until tender, about one hour. Remove from the heat and allow to cool. When cold, remove the bones and dice meat into neat cubes.

Combine the goat, onions, chives and spring onions, season to taste, then add the lime juice and lastly the coconut cream. If canned coconut cream is not available add 2½ cups of hot water to 2 cups of desiccated coconut. Stir well and allow to cool. Knead for a few minutes and then strain through a muslin cloth.

An attractive serving idea is to halve lengthways 3 red peppers (capsicum), remove the seeds and spoon the goat inside. Serve each half as an entrée portion.

Roast Leg of Goat with Garlic Sauce

TIME TO ALLOW: 1 hour
SERVES 6

1 leg of goat, about 3 pounds (1.5 kg)
3 cloves of garlic, peeled and sliced lengthways
oil
seasoning
½ pint (300 ml) hot water or vegetable stock

With a sharp, thin knife make several small incisions in the goat. Press the garlic pieces into these holes, rub the leg with salt, freshly ground black pepper, and oil.

Place the meat in a roasting tray and roast in a moderately hot oven (400°F/205°C/gas regulo 6) for approximately 40 minutes, basting frequently. The slightly pink meat is juicy and tender.

Remove from the oven and pour the water or vegetable stock into the roasting tray and bring to the boil on an element. Simmer for 5 minutes then remove the meat to a serving dish. Season the roasting tray juices and pour into a sauce boat. Serve.

Roast Leg of Goat with Citrus Fruit

TIME TO ALLOW: 1¼ hours
SERVES 6

1 leg of goat, about 3 pounds (1.5 kg)
1 lemon, peeled and sliced thinly
2 oranges, peeled and sliced thinly
1 ounce (25 g) sugar
oil
seasoning
1 pint (600 ml) water or vegetable stock
2 ounces (50 g) butter
2 ounces (50 g) flour

Place the meat in a roasting tray, season with salt and freshly ground black pepper, and cover evenly with the slices of orange and lemon. Sprinkle with the oil and sugar.

Add the water (or vegetable stock) to the roasting tray and cover with foil. Roast in a moderate oven (375°F/190°C/gas regulo 4-5) for approximately 40 minutes. When done, remove the goat from the dish and keep warm. (If the meat feels tough when pierced with a skewer it may require more cooking.)

Melt the butter in a saucepan and add the flour. Cook for a few minutes then allow to cool before adding the juices from the roasting tray. Stir in briskly to avoid lumps, bring to the boil, season to taste, and if necessary, thin with water. Pour into a sauce boat for serving.

Goat Goulash with Sauerkraut

TIME TO ALLOW: 1 hour
SERVES 6

2 pounds (1 kg) boneless shoulder of goat, diced
2 medium onions, chopped finely
1 teaspoooon paprika
¼ pint (150 ml) white vinegar
8 ounces (200 g) prepared sauerkraut
1 clove garlic, crushed
1 pinch caraway seeds
pinch each of thyme and marjoram
½ pint (300 ml) sour cream
oil for frying
seasoning

Fry the onions gently in oil in a heavy-bottomed saucepan. Add the paprika and continue to fry on a low heat for 2-3 minutes, then add the goat, season, and cook for a further 2-3 minutes. Add the white vinegar, then place a lid on the saucepan and simmer gently for 30-45 minutes, or until tender.

Stir in the sauerkraut and heat through.

Mix the garlic, caraway seeds, thyme and marjoram to a paste and add to the goulash. Lastly, add the sour cream and correct the seasoning.

Curried Goat

TIME TO ALLOW: 1-1½ hours
SERVES 4-6

2 pounds (1 kg) boneless shoulder of goat, diced
1 ounce (25 g) butter
1 ounce (25 g) flour
2 medium onions, chopped finely
1 clove garlic, crushed
2 medium apples, chopped finely
1 teaspoon curry powder
3 cloves, finely ground
2 tablespoons tomato paste
¼ pint (150 ml) coconut cream
¼ pint (150 ml) pineapple juice
seasoning

Melt the butter in a heavy-bottomed saucepan, add the onions, curry powder and garlic, and fry for a few minutes. Add the apples and ground cloves. While this is cooking gently, dust the goat pieces evenly with flour, then add to the pan, season, and fry for a further 10 minutes. Mix in the tomato paste, coconut cream and pineapple juice. If there is not enough liquid to just cover the meat, add a little water.

Cover the saucepan and simmer the curry until the meat is tender, about 30 minutes. Correct the seasoning before serving. Serve the curry with a suitable accompaniment such as mango chutney and plain rice.

Older goat can be used in this recipe but cook it a little longer.

Goat and Vegetable Stew

TIME TO ALLOW: 2½ hours
SERVES 4 to 6

2 pounds (1 kg) boneless shoulder of goat, diced
1 ounce (25 g) flour
1 clove garlic, crushed
1 ounce (25 g) tomato paste
24 small onions, peeled
8 ounces (200 g) carrots, peeled and diced
8 ounces (200 g) turnips, peeled and diced
1 pound (450 g) small new potatoes
3 spring onions cut into 1 inch (2.5 cm) lengths
oil
water

Brown the goat in a heavy-bottomed frying pan on a high heat, sprinkle with flour and fry with the garlic until light brown in colour. Add the water so that the meat is just covered, season and add the tomato paste. Braise slowly for 1½ hours.

Add the peeled onions, carrots and turnips cut into 1 inch (2.5 cm) dices, and the potatoes, and cook for a further 20 minutes until the meat and vegetables are tender.

Skim off any fat from the sauce and add the spring onions just before serving.

Boiled Shoulder of Goat with Watercress Sauce

TIME TO ALLOW: 1½-2 hours
SERVES 4 to 6

1 shoulder of goat, about 3 pounds (1.5 kg)
2 medium onions, peeled and sliced roughly
1 medium carrot, peeled and sliced roughly
2 stalks of celery, sliced
12 black peppercorns
seasoning
¼ pint (150 ml) cream
4 ounces (100 g) butter
4 ounces (100 g) flour
water
1 pound (450 g) watercress, washed, with leaves separated.

Place the goat, onions, carrot, celery, peppercorns and salt in a large saucepan. Top up with water and bring to the boil. Simmer until tender, about 1 hour. Remove meat and keep warm.

Melt the butter in a saucepan, add the flour and cook for a few minutes. Allow to cool slightly before adding 1½ pints (900 ml) of the strained cooking liquor. Bring the mixture to the boil, add the watercress stalks, and simmer for 10 minutes. Correct the seasoning, strain the sauce and add the watercress leaves and cream before serving.

Slice the meat and coat with the sauce.

Loin of Goat with Sweet Potato Purée

TIME TO ALLOW: 45 minutes
SERVES 4

2 loins of goat, each about 1 pound (450 g), boned and trimmed
1 pound (450 g) sweet potatoes
1 ounce (25 g) butter
1/8 pint (75 ml) milk
oil
seasoning
pinch of nutmeg

Wash, peel and boil the sweet potatoes until cooked.

Lay the loins of goat flat in a roasting tray, season and rub over with oil, and roast in a moderately hot oven (400°F/205°C/gas regulo 6) for 10 minutes. Remove from the oven, leaving the loins in the tray.

Drain and mash the sweet potatoes thoroughly, adding butter, then milk, seasoning and nutmeg. Mash until the texture is smooth taking care not to make mixture too wet. Spread this mixture evenly over the loins and replace in the oven for 10 minutes at above temperature, then cook for a further 10 minutes on grill (or turn top element to high and bottom element off) until quite crisp on top.

Transfer to a serving dish and serve.

This dish can be prepared beforehand so that only the last 20 minutes of cooking needs to be done before carving and serving.

Goat Chops Baked in Cream

TIME TO ALLOW: 30 minutes
SERVES 6

12 goat chops, each about 4 ounces (100 g)
1 medium onion, sliced thinly
1 capsicum, seeded and sliced thinly
oil for frying
flour
seasoning
¼ pint (150 ml) white wine
¾ pint (450 ml) cream

Trim the chops and dust with flour. Fry the onion and capsicum gently in oil in a large roasting dish. Add the floured chops, season, and fry for a few minutes on each side. Add the wine and half the cream.

Place in the oven and bake at a moderate heat (375°F/190°C/gas regulo 4-5) for 20 minutes, or until tender.

Remove the chops from the pan and keep warm. Add the remaining cream to the pan, bring to the boil and taste to correct the seasoning.

Pour the sauce over the chops to serve.

Crumbed Goat Cutlets

TIME TO ALLOW: 20-30 minutes
SERVES 6

12 goat cutlets, each about 4 ounces (100 g)
flour
egg
breadcrumbs
seasoning
oil

Trim the cutlets and carefully remove all the bone apart from the rib. Beat the meat lightly with a wooden mallet.

Season the flour with salt and pepper and crumb the cutlets by passing them through the seasoned flour, shaking off the surplus, then dipping them in the beaten egg mixed with milk and, finally, patting on the breadcrumbs firmly.

Heat the oil in a heavy-bottomed frying pan and fry the cutlets for 4-5 minutes on each side. Drain cutlets on a paper towel before serving to remove any excess fat.

Spiced Goat Loaf

TIME TO ALLOW: 1 hour
SERVES 4 to 6

2 pounds (1 kg) boned and minced goat
1 generous pinch each of ginger, turmeric, paprika and cayenne
½ ounce (12 g) flour
1 egg, beaten lightly
seasoning

LIQUID FOR STEAMING
1½ pints (1 litre) water
1 large sprig of thyme
1 bunch coriander

SAUCE
1 medium onion, chopped finely
oil for frying
1 teaspoon paprika
½ teaspoon coriander
¼ pint (150 ml) yoghurt

Combine the minced meat with the spices and flour and season with salt and freshly ground black pepper. Add the egg and mix well. Form into a loaf shape and place in a greased dish just large enough to hold the mixture.

Put the water, thyme and coriander in a steamer and bring to the boil. Place the meat dish in the steamer and steam for 25-30 minutes. (If a steamer is not available a large dish placed on the element and covered with foil will suffice.)

Sauté the onion in oil, season lightly and add the paprika and coriander. When the onion is tender add the juices from the loaf and then add the yoghurt. Heat through and pour over the loaf to serve.

Saddle of Goat with Blackcurrant Sauce

TIME TO ALLOW: 4 hours for marinating, 1 hour for cooking
SERVES 4 to 5

1 saddle of goat, about 3 pounds (1.5 kg)
1 pint (600 ml) white wine
1/8 pint (75 ml) Creme de Cassis (blackcurrant liqueur)
1 pound (500 g) blackcurrants
oil
seasoning
pinch of sugar
3 ounces (75 g) flour

Trim the saddle of goat carefully and place in a deep dish. (If the saddle is too large for the dish, cut in half at the end of the ribs). Pour the wine and liqueur over the meat and marinate for 4 hours, turning the meat every hour or so. Alternatively the meat can be left to marinate overnight.

Remove the goat from the marinade and pat dry with a clean cloth. Place the meat in a roasting tray, season, and rub over with oil. Roast in a moderately hot oven (400°F/205°C/gas regulo 6) for 30-45 minutes. Remove meat and keep it warm while the sauce is made.

Mix the flour to a smooth paste with the pan juices. Heat the marinade and pour into the pan, then add the blackcurrants, a pinch of sugar and the seasoning. Bring to the boil slowly and simmer for about 15 minutes. Taste to correct the seasoning, then pass the sauce through a sieve and serve in a sauce boat.

Duck and Chinese Date Soup

TIME TO ALLOW: 2 hours
SERVES 6

1 duck, about 1½ pounds (650 g) (Use one unsuitable for roasting)
2 pints (1200 ml) water
1 medium onion, chopped
1 medium carrot, chopped
1 stick celery, chopped
2 bay leaves

8 ounces (200 g) dried Chinese dates
2 ounces (50 g) butter
2 ounces (50 g) flour
seasoning

Put the duck into a large saucepan with the water, chopped vegetables and bay leaves. Bring to the boil, then simmer for 1½ hours, skimming the surface from time to time. Remove the duck, slice the meat, and set aside.

Melt the butter in a saucepan, add the flour and cook for a few minutes. Cool slightly, then strain in the hot stock, stirring continuously to avoid lumps. Bring slowly to the boil.

Meanwhile, boil the dates in water until reconstituted, about 20 minutes. Pit the dates, slice roughly, and add to the soup, together with the sliced meat from the duck. Taste to correct the seasoning.

Roast Wild Duck with Liver Stuffing

TIME TO ALLOW: 1½ hours
SERVES 4 to 6

2 ducks, each about 1-1½ pounds (450-650 g)
1 large onion, chopped finely
1 clove garlic, crushed
12 ounces (300 g) livers (chicken and duck)
4 ounces (100 g) fatty bacon
1 egg
1 pint (600 ml) hot stock
2 ounces (50 g) flour
oil
seasoning

Mince the livers and bacon finely and mix with the chopped onion and garlic. Season, then add an egg. Mix a little more, then divide the mixture in half and place inside the ducks. The stuffing can be held inside by using a crust of bread.

Rub the ducks with oil and season lightly. Place in a roasting dish and roast in a moderate oven (375°F/190°C/gas regulo 4-5) for about 1 hour, until the breasts are just pink throughout. Remove the ducks and keep warm.

Mix the flour to a fine paste with the roasting dish juices and cook for a few minutes. Cool slightly, then add the hot stock. Bring to the boil and season to taste. Strain the sauce into a sauce boat to serve.

Roast Wild Duck with Black Cherry Sauce

TIME TO ALLOW: 1½ hours
SERVES 4

2 ducks, each about 1-1½ pounds (450-650 g)
1 orange
2 bay leaves
¼ pint (150 ml) Kirsch
1 pint (600 ml) hot stock
1 pound (450 g) can black morello cherries, drained
oil
seasoning
pinch of sugar
2 ounces (50 g) flour

Place half an orange and one bay leaf inside each duck. Put the ducks in a roasting tray, season and rub with oil. Roast in a moderate oven (375°F/190°C/gas regulo 4-5) for about 1 hour until pink throughout. Remove the ducks and keep warm.

Stir the flour into the roasting-tray juices, mixing to a smooth paste. Add the hot stock and half the cherries. Bring slowly to the boil and season with salt, pepper and a little sugar. Simmer for about 15 minutes, then strain into a clean saucepan. Add the remaining cherries, return to the boil then add the Kirsch. Simmer a little longer, correct the seasoning, and serve over the ducks.

Roast Duck with Wild Rice Stuffing

TIME TO ALLOW: 2 hours
SERVES 4

2 ducks, each about 1½ pounds (650 g)
4 ounces (100 g) wild rice
1 large onion, chopped finely
1 clove garlic, crushed
livers and giblets, chopped
1 egg
2 ounces (50 g) flour
oil
seasoning
1 small bunch fresh basil
1 pint (600 ml) hot stock

Boil the rice in plenty of water until just tender, about 17 minutes, and wash under cold water. Strain. Long-grained rice may be substituted for wild rice if desired.

Fry the onion, garlic, livers and giblets in oil and add to the rice. Mix in an egg and season to taste. Place the stuffing inside the ducks. Rub the ducks with oil and season and place in a roasting tray. Roast in a moderate oven (375°F/190°C/gas regulo 4-5) for 1 hour, or until light pink throughout. Remove the ducks and keep warm.

Mix the flour to a smooth paste with the pan juices. Add the stock, stirring constantly to avoid lumps, then bring to the boil and season to taste.

Pull the leaves from the basil and place the stalks in the sauce. Cook slowly for 5-10 minutes, then strain sauce into a clean saucepan. Slice the basil leaves thinly and add them to the strained sauce. Correct the seasoning and pour over the ducks before serving.

Roast Wild Duck with Mustard and Lemon

TIME TO ALLOW: 1½ hours
SERVES 4

2 ducks, each about 1-1½ pounds (450-650 g)
3 tablespoons prepared mild French mustard
juice from 2 lemons
1 clove garlic, crushed
1 pint (600 ml) stock or water
2 ounces (50 g) flour
seasoning

Mix the mustard, garlic and lemon juice together and rub the ducks with this mixture. Sprinkle with salt and freshly ground black pepper and place in a roasting tray. Cover with foil and roast in a moderate oven (375°F/190°C/gas regulo 4-5) for an hour, until the breasts are cooked but slightly pink. Remove the ducks and keep warm.

Mix the flour to a smooth paste with the roasting juices and cook for a few minutes. Cool slightly, then add the hot stock, stirring all the time. Season, bring to the boil, then simmer for a few minutes. Strain the sauce into a sauce boat and serve separately.

Wild Duck with Cider

TIME TO ALLOW: 1½ hours
SERVES 4

2 ducks, each about 1½ pounds (650 g)
4 ounces (100 g) butter
2 pints (1200 ml) dry cider
⅛ pint (75 ml) Calvados
2 pounds (1 kg) sour apples
¼ pint (150 ml) cream
seasoning

Melt the butter in a roasting dish and place the ducks in. Season, and brown in a hot oven (425°F/220°C/gas regulo 7) for about 40 minutes. Remove from the oven, pour in the Calvados and flame, then cook for a few minutes. Add the cider and bring to the boil. Remove the ducks and keep warm. Reduce the cooking liquor by half. Add the cream and reduce by a further one-third.

Return the duck to the pan and cook for 10 minutes. Peel and quarter the apples and add them to the sauce, cooking until tender.

Place the ducks on a serving dish and surround with the cooked apples. Pour the cider sauce over to serve.

Wild Duck with Olives

TIME TO ALLOW: 2 hours
SERVES 4

2 wild ducks, each about 1½ pounds (650 g)
2 large onions, chopped
½ pint (300 ml) Madeira
3 dozen olives, pitted
3 ounces (75 g) tomato paste
1 clove garlic, crushed
1 pint (600 ml) stock or water
3 ounces (75 g) flour
1 ounce (25 g) parsley, chopped
oil
seasoning

Heat some oil in a large casserole dish and brown the ducks on all sides. Add the onions and garlic, cook for a few minutes, then add the flour, mixing to a smooth paste with the onions and oil. Blend in the tomato paste slowly, cook for 2-3 minutes, then add the Madeira and hot stock. Stir well, and season. Cover the dish with a tight-fitting lid, and cook in a moderate oven (375°F/190°C/gas regulo 4-5) until tender, about 1-1½ hours. Just prior to serving, add the stoned olives and the parsley.

Serve from the casserole, spooning the sauce over each portion.

This dish is suitable for older ducks, as they become tender with the slow braising in the oven, without being stringy.

Wild Duck with Brown Onion Sauce

TIME TO ALLOW: 1½ hours
SERVES 4

2 ducks, each about 1½ pounds (650 g)
3 large onions, shredded
1 clove garlic, crushed
flour
oil
seasoning
pinch of sugar
½ pint (300 ml) red wine
½ pint (300 ml) water or stock

Joint the ducks into legs and breasts, dust with flour and brown in oil in a deep heavy-bottomed frying pan. Remove and keep warm.

Add the onions to the frying pan and continue to fry until quite brown. Add the garlic, sugar and seasoning, cook for a few minutes, then return the duck portions. Season and add the wine and just enough water to cover the ducks. Cover the pan with a tight-fitting lid and cook on a low heat until the duck is tender, about 45-60 minutes.

Casseroled Duck

TIME TO ALLOW: 2½ hours
SERVES 6 to 8

2 ducks, each about 1½ pounds (650 g)
2 stalks celery, chopped
2 carrots, sliced
2 large onions, sliced
¼ pint (150 ml) brandy
¾ pint (450 ml) red wine
6 ounces (150 g) fatty bacon, diced
1 clove garlic, crushed
8 ounces (200 g) mushrooms
oil
seasoning

Joint the duck into serving pieces and place in a porcelain or earthenware bowl. Add the seasoning, celery, onions, carrots, brandy and wine. Marinate for 2 hours.

Remove the duck from the marinade, drain, and pat dry on a paper towel. Sauté the diced bacon in oil until golden, remove from pan, then brown the duck pieces. Place the duck and bacon in a casserole and cook for 20 minutes in a moderate oven (375°F/190°C/gas regulo 4-5).

Add the marinade, garlic and mushrooms to the casserole and cook for a further 1½ hours on a low heat (220°F/100°C/gas regulo 1).

Skim off the fat, taste to correct the seasoning and serve in the casserole.

Aubergine with Duck Stuffing

TIME TO ALLOW: 1½ hours
SERVES 8

2 ducks, each about 1½ pounds (650 g)
1 medium onion, chopped finely
1 clove garlic, crushed
1 green pepper, seeded and chopped
2 medium tomatoes, skinned, seeded and chopped
4 aubergines
½ pint (300 ml) white wine
oil
seasoning

Rub the ducks with oil and season lightly. Place in a roasting dish and roast in a moderate oven (375°F/190°C/gas regulo 4-5) for about 1 hour, until the flesh is just pink throughout. Remove from the oven, and when cool enough to handle remove the meat from the bones and dice.

Skin the tomatoes. (Remove the core and make a small cross in the skin at the opposite end. Plunge into boiling water for 7-8 seconds, then run under cold water. The skin can now be removed easily.) Cut each tomato in half and remove the seeds.

Cut the aubergines in half lengthways and remove the flesh, taking care not to damage the skins. Dice the flesh and set aside.

Fry the onions and garlic in oil and when nearly tender add the green pepper, tomatoes and diced aubergine. Cook for a few minutes, then add the duck meat. Season, then add the wine and continue cooking until the aubergine is tender.

Spoon the mixture into the aubergine shells, brush with oil and bake in a moderately hot oven (400°F/205°C/gas regulo 6) for 15 minutes.

See photograph opposite p.105

Simple Duck Pâté

Older ducks have a strong flavour which is well suited to this simple pâté.

TIME TO ALLOW: 3½ hours
SERVES 8

2 ducks, each about 3 pounds (1.5 kg)
1 large onion, sliced thinly
1 clove garlic, crushed
parsley, chopped
seasoning
oil
pinch of allspice
¼ pint (150 ml) fresh cream

Rub the ducks with oil and place them in a deep roasting dish. Season, cover with foil or a tight-fitting lid, and roast in a slow oven (275°F/135°C/gas regulo 2) until tender, about 2-3 hours. Remove from the oven and pour off the pan juices and reserve. Cook the onion and garlic in the roasting dish until tender.

Bone the ducks and mince on a fine blade, together with the onion and garlic. Season with salt and freshly ground black pepper, and add a pinch of allspice, the finely chopped parsley and the cream. Skim the duck fat from the reserved roasting tray juices before adding to the duck.

Blend thoroughly, taste to correct seasoning, and pour into individual dishes, or into a large terrine dish. Chill.

Serve with toast.

Duck and Mint Salad

TIME TO ALLOW: 30 minutes
SERVES 4

1 pound (450 g) cooked and boned duck, cut into fingers
4 ounces (100 g) celery shoots
4 ounces (100 g) white grapes
2 oranges, segmented
1 large bunch fresh mint, chopped roughly
¼ pint (150 ml) prepared mayonnaise
seasoning

Mix the mint with a little sugar to make it easier to chop. Combine all the ingredients, mixing lightly. Season to taste and allow to stand for 10 minutes before serving.

GOOSE

HUNTING SEASON

1st September-31st January. (There is an extension to February 20 for certain areas.)

Wild goose should be hung by its neck for one to three days and will be ready to pluck and draw when the tail feathers pull out readily. Old birds take longer than young birds to reach this stage.

Geese live entirely on grass and other vegetation and the flesh is never tainted as can sometimes happen with duck.

Unlike most game birds, geese are very fatty. A roasted goose will yield a large amount of fat which keeps well in the refrigerator and can be used for cooking. It gives a splendid flavour to sautéed meats and vegetables, pâtés and casseroles. Frequent skimming of the dish is recommended for removing excess fat when the goose is cooked by any method other than roasting.

Livers from wild geese are tasty and can be used in stuffings and sauces. A pâté made from liver will be more easily digestible with the addition of a little goose fat.

Roast Goose with Green and Red Peppers

TIME TO ALLOW: 2½ hours
SERVES 6

1 goose, about 8 pounds (4 kg)
3 peppers (capsicum), green and red, seeded and sliced
1 large onion, sliced
1 clove garlic, crushed
1 teaspoon paprika
oil
flour
seasoning
1 pint (600 ml) hot stock or water

Season and roast the goose in a moderate oven (375°F/190°C/gas regulo 4-5) for 1½-2 hours, or until tender. Transfer the goose to a serving dish and keep warm.

Pour nearly all the fat from the roasting dish, then add the garlic and paprika. Fry for a few minutes, then sprinkle with a little flour and add the onions and peppers. Continue frying for a few minutes, gradually adding the hot stock, stirring all the time. Bring to the boil and season to taste. Simmer for 10 minutes, then pour the sauce over the goose.

Roast Goose with Fruit Stuffing

TIME TO ALLOW: 3 hours
SERVES 6

1 goose, dressed, about 6 pounds (3 kg)
8 cooking apples
12 ounces (300 g) mixed sultanas and currants
4 ounces (100 g) fine breadcrumbs
2 beaten eggs
pinch of cinnamon
2 ounces (50 g) flour
stock or vegetable water

Peel and core the apples and segment them evenly. Mix with the other ingredients. Season lightly and place the stuffing inside the goose.

Place the goose in a roasting dish with ½ pint (300 ml) of water, rub with oil, and season. Roast in a moderate oven (375°F/190°C/gas regulo 4-5) for 2-2½ hours or until tender. (An older goose may need longer cooking, but a young gosling can take as little as 1½ hours.)

Remove the goose on to a serving dish and keep warm while you make the gravy.

Pour off the goose fat from the roasting tray and mix the residue with the flour. Cook a little, then add stock or vegetable water, bring to the boil and season.

A suitable accompaniment for this dish would be potato dumplings, braised red cabbage, and apple sauce.

Roast Goose with Muscat Grape Sauce

TIME TO ALLOW: 2½ hours
SERVES 6

1 goose, about 8 pounds (4 kg)
1 apple, halved
1 orange, halved
½ pint (300 ml) white wine
2 ounces (50 g) flour
¾ pint (450 ml) hot stock or water
½ pint (300 ml) Curaçao (or other orange liqueur)
½ pound (200 g) muscat grapes
seasoning

Place the apples and oranges inside the goose, season, and place it in a roasting tray. Pour in the wine and roast in a moderate oven (375°F/190°C/gas regulo 4-5) for 1½-2 hours, or until the goose is tender. When the goose is done transfer it to a serving dish and keep warm while preparing the sauce.

Pour off most of the goose fat from the roasting tray, and mix the flour to a smooth paste with the remaining fat and pan juices. Cook for a few minutes, cool slightly, then add the hot stock, stirring all the time. Season, and bring to the boil.

While the goose is cooking, peel and remove the pips from the grapes and place in a saucepan with the Curaçao. Heat gently, then ignite to flame the liqueur. When the flames die down, strain the gravy into the grapes, taste to correct the seasoning, and serve with the goose.

Roast Goose with Potato Stuffing

TIME TO ALLOW: 2½ hours
SERVES 6

1 goose, about 8 pounds (4 kg)
1 pound (450 g) potatoes, washed and peeled
1 onion, chopped finely
1 clove garlic, crushed
1 egg
seasoning
pinch of nutmeg

Boil the potatoes until tender, drain, then mash thoroughly. Season with salt, pepper and a pinch of nutmeg. Add the diced onion and crushed garlic, and finally the egg, making sure it is all well mixed. Taste to correct the seasoning then place inside the goose and secure with string. Season the goose and roast in a moderate oven (375°F/190°C/gas regulo 4-5) for 1½-2 hours, or until tender.

Serve with a garnish of sauerkraut and a roast gravy. A little white vinegar added to the gravy will give it a piquant taste.

Roast Goose with Caraway Sauce

TIME TO ALLOW: 2½ hours
SERVES 6

1 goose, about 8 pounds (4 kg)
1 pint (600 ml) stock or water
2 ounces (50 g) flour
⅛ pint (75 ml) kummel liqueur (caraway flavour)
1 ounce (25 g) caraway seeds)
1 clove garlic, crushed   )   mixed together
pinch marjoram   )
seasoning

Place the goose in a roasting tray and season. Roast in a moderate oven (375°F/190°C/gas regulo 4-5) until tender — about 1½-2 hours. Transfer the goose to a serving tray and keep warm.

Pour all but a little fat from the roasting tray and then mix the remaining fat with the flour to a smooth paste, cook a few minutes, then cool slightly before adding the hot stock, stirring constantly. Bring to the boil, season, and simmer for a few minutes. Add the liqueur and lastly the garlic, caraway and marjoram mixture. Taste to correct the seasoning, then pour the sauce over the goose.

Roast Goose with Pineapple and Peppercorns

TIME TO ALLOW: 2½ hours
SERVES 6

1 goose, about 8 pounds (4 kg)
6 slices fresh pineapple, cored and skinned (or canned pineapple slices)
12 black peppercorns, cracked
½ pint (300 ml) pineapple juice
½ pint (300 ml) hot stock
2 ounces (50 g) flour
2 cloves garlic, crushed
seasoning

Place the pineapple trimmings (if fresh pineapple is used) inside the goose, season, and roast in a moderate oven (375°F/190°C/gas regulo 4-5) for 1½-2 hours, or until tender. Remove the goose and keep warm.

Pour off the fat from the roasting tray and add the flour to the remaining juices. Mix to a smooth paste, then add the stock and pineapple juice, stirring to avoid lumps. Bring the sauce to the boil and season to taste, then strain in to a clean saucepan and add the pineapple slices. Heat the sauce through.

Carve the goose and place a slice of pineapple on each portion, pour over the sauce and sprinkle with the cracked pepper.

Roast Goose with Apple and Prune Stuffing

TIME TO ALLOW: 2½ hours
SERVES 6

1 goose, about 8 pounds (4 kg)
1 pound (450 g) apples
6 ounces (150 g) prunes
1 ounce (25 g) brown sugar
zest of 1 lemon

Soak the prunes in warm water for 15 minutes, then drain, remove the stones and dice. Peel and core the apples, then dice and mix with the prunes. Add the brown sugar and lemon zest and blend thoroughly.

Place the stuffing inside the goose and secure with string. Place in a roasting tray, season, then roast in a moderate oven (375°F/190°C/gas regulo 4-5) for 1½-2 hours, or until tender.

Roast Goose with Chestnut Stuffing

TIME TO ALLOW: 2½ hours
SERVES 6

1 goose, about 8 pounds (4 kg)
1 medium onion, chopped finely
8 ounces (200 g) can chestnut purée
1 clove garlic, crushed
1 apple, peeled, cored and grated
oil
seasoning

Fry the onion in a little oil until transparent, then add the crushed garlic and fry a little longer. Add the chestnut purée and apple and mix thoroughly without further cooking. Place the stuffing inside the goose and secure with string. Season the goose and roast in a moderate oven (375°F/190°F/gas regulo 4-5) for 1½-2 hours, or until tender. Transfer the goose to a serving dish.

Roast Goose with Sausage Meat Stuffing

TIME TO ALLOW: 2½ hours
SERVES 6

1 goose, about 8 pounds (4 kg)
1 large onion, chopped finely
oil or fat for frying
8 ounces (200 g) sausage meat
small bunch parsley, chopped finely
3 anchovy fillets, pounded
2 eggs
juice from half a lemon
8 ounces (200 g) livers (preferably from the goose), chopped
2 ounces (50 g) dry breadcrumbs
pinch each of thyme and tarragon
seasoning

Fry the livers in a little oil for a few minutes then set aside. Pan-fry the onion until transparent, then add the sausage meat and sauté until light brown. Add the livers and all the other ingredients to the mixture and blend lightly. Place inside the goose and secure with string.

Season and place the goose in a roasting tray. Sprinkle with flour and roast in a hot oven (425°F/220°C/gas regulo 7) for 15 minutes, then reduce the heat to 350°F (175°C/gas regulo 3) and continue to roast until the goose is tender, about 2 hours.

A plain roast gravy made from the roasting pan juices and stock is best with this stuffing.

Cold Sliced Goose with Spicy Rice Salad

TIME TO ALLOW: 30 minutes for salad, with cooked goose and prepared mayonnaise
SERVES 8

1 goose, about 8 pounds (4 kg)
12 ounces (300 g) long grain rice
1 red pepper (capsicum), seeded and diced
1 onion, chopped finely
2 gherkins, chopped finely
¼ pint (150 ml) mango chutney
4 ounces (100 g) diced or crushed pineapple
pinch cayenne pepper
pinch saffron
½ pint (300 ml) well-flavoured mayonnaise
½ teaspoon turmeric
½ teaspoon garam masala
1 tablespoon desiccated coconut
¼ pint (150 ml) cream
juice from half a lemon
seasoning

Roast the goose in a moderate oven (375°F/190°C/gas regulo 4-5) for 1½-2 hours, or until tender. Allow to cool, then remove the bones and cut the meat into neat slices. This can be done well in advance.

Boil the rice in plenty of well-salted water to which a pinch of saffron has been added. When the rice is just tender, about 15 minutes, drain, rinse under cold water and drain well.

Put the rice into a salad bowl with the onions, pepper, gherkins and pineapple. Mix together lightly, then season, adding a pinch of cayenne, then the mango chutney. Taste to correct the seasoning and set aside.

Blend the turmeric and garam masala with the coconut and cream and add the lemon juice. Mix in the mayonnaise and leave to stand for one hour.

Serve the goose with the rice salad and the spicy mayonnaise served separately.

Boiled Goose with Bread Sauce

TIME TO ALLOW: 2 hours
SERVES 6

1 goose, about 7-8 pounds (3.5-4 kg)
3 medium onions, sliced
3 sticks celery, sliced
2 bay leaves
3 cloves
1½ pints (900 ml) milk
4 cloves garlic, peeled
6 black peppercorns
4 ounces (100 g) breadcrumbs
6 egg yolks
¼ pint (150 ml) cream
pinch of nutmeg
seasoning

Place the goose in a saucepan, cover with water and bring to the boil. Skim, then add the sliced onion and celery, one bay leaf and cloves, and season. Simmer until the goose is tender, about 1½ hours.

Meanwhile, bring the milk to the boil with the garlic, peppercorns and the other bay leaf. Simmer until the garlic is thoroughly tender, strain, then add the breadcrumbs and season to taste. Mix the egg yolks with the cream and add to the hot milk, whisking continuously. Return to the heat and bring to boiling point, but do not boil or the egg yolks will curdle. Taste to correct seasoning and add a pinch of nutmeg.

Remove the goose from the stock and place on a serving dish. Serve the sauce separately.

Keep the stock from the goose as a base for soup.

Sautéed Goose Livers

TIME TO ALLOW: 30 minutes for marinating, 10 minutes for cooking
SERVES 4 entrées

1 pound (450 g) goose livers
½ pint (300 ml) milk
1 clove garlic, crushed

1 medium onion, chopped finely
2 rashers bacon, chopped
¼ pint (150 ml) sherry
oil
seasoning

Check the livers to ensure they are cleaned and trimmed properly (i.e. no galls), then marinate them in the milk and crushed garlic for 30 minutes. Remove from marinade and pat dry.

Heat a heavy-bottomed frying pan with a little oil and fry the onions until golden. Add the bacon and cook for 2-3 minutes, then add the livers. Season, and continue to sauté for 6-7 minutes. Add the sherry and set alight. When the flames have died down, taste to correct the seasoning and serve.

Goose and Grapefruit Salad

TIME TO ALLOW: 2½ hours for roasting, 20 minutes for salad preparation
SERVES 6, or 10 as an appetiser

1 goose, about 8 pounds (4 kg)
4 grapefruit
small bunch chives, cut into 1 inch (2.5 cm) lengths
1 red pepper (capsicum) seeded and sliced

DRESSING
½ pint (300 ml) prepared mayonnaise
juice from 1 grapefruit
seasoning

Season the goose, then roast in a moderate oven (375°F/190°C/gas regulo 4-5) for 1½-2 hours, or until tender. Allow to cool, then remove the bones and cut the meat into bite-sized pieces.

Scoop the flesh from the grapefruit and mix with the chives, red pepper and goose meat. Season with salt and freshly ground black pepper.

Mix the grapefruit juice in with the mayonnaise and add to the salad. Blend lightly.

This salad is suitable for a light luncheon or as a separate course for a formal dinner.

Goose and Watercress Soup

Use the bones from a roast goose dinner to prepare this simple soup.

TIME TO ALLOW: 2 hours
SERVES 6

goose bones and trimmings
2 pints (1200 ml) water
8 ounces (200 g) vegetables (carrot, onion, celery, leek)
1 bay leaf
6 peppercorns
2 ounces (50 g) butter
2 ounces (50 g) flour
8 ounces (200 g) watercress, washed and chopped
seasoning

Bring the bones to boil in the water, skim, then add the chopped vegetables, bay leaf and peppercorns. Simmer gently for 1-1½ hours.

Melt the butter in a saucepan, then add the flour. Cook for 2-3 minutes, then gradually add the strained hot stock, stirring all the time. Season and return to the boil. Finally, add the watercress and simmer for a few minutes. Taste to correct seasoning.

PHEASANT

HUNTING SEASON
1st October-1st February

Pheasant needs to be hung longer than most other game birds to allow its distinctive flavour to develop. Birds should be hung by their necks in a cool airy place from seven to fourteen days.

Pheasant that has been aged carefully has a highly-flavoured and tender flesh. Many people consider it ready for eating just as it starts to decompose.

A good poulterer will supply a bird or a brace of the requisite degree of gaminess — fairly fresh or well hung — ready to eat on a given date.

The hen pheasant has a more delicate flavour than the cock, and a young bird, distinguished by a pliable beak and rounded spurs, can be cooked most successfully.

All pheasant has a tendency to be somewhat dry and it should never be overcooked.

Pheasant Stock

Use the bones from a pheasant dinner or an old bird unsuitable for cooking as the basis for the stock.

TIME TO ALLOW: 2 hours

Pheasant bones and trimmings
2 pints (1200 ml) water
1 medium onion, chopped
1 medium carrot, chopped
1 stick celery, chopped
1 bay leaf
6 peppercorns

Bring the bones to boil in the water, skim, then add the chopped vegetables, bay leaf and peppercorns. Simmer gently for 1½-2 hours. Strain.

Pheasant and Leek Soup

TIME TO ALLOW: 45 minutes, from prepared stock
SERVES 4

2 pints (1200 ml) hot pheasant stock
2 ounces (50 g) butter
2 ounces (50 g) flour
8 ounces (200 g) leeks, washed, trimmed and sliced thinly
4 ounces (100 g) cooked pheasant, cut into thin strips
4 ounces (100 g) pitted prunes, cut into thin strips

Melt the butter in a saucepan and add the flour. Cook for a few minutes without colouring, then add the hot stock, stirring briskly to avoid lumps. Bring to the boil, add the leeks, and season to taste. Simmer for 15 minutes, then add the cooked pheasant and prunes. Taste to correct seasoning, then return to the boil and serve.

Chilled Pheasant and Avocado Soup

TIME TO ALLOW: 30 minutes from prepared stock
SERVES 8

2 pints (1200 ml) cold pheasant stock
8 ounces (200 g) cooked pheasant, diced
4 ripe avocados
1 clove garlic, crushed
pinch cayenne
seasoning
⅛ pint (75 ml) white vinegar
¼ pint (150 ml) olive oil

Halve the avocados and scoop out the flesh. Mix with the cold pheasant stock, garlic, cayenne and seasoning and blend thoroughly. Add the oil and vinegar, taste to correct the seasoning, then add the pheasant meat.
  Chill well before serving.

Steamed Pheasant with Papaya

TIME TO ALLOW: 45 minutes
SERVES 6 to 8

2 pheasant, each about 2 pounds (1 kg)
½ papaya
juice from 2 oranges
juice from half a lemon
⅛ pint (75 ml) Grand Marnier (or orange liqueur)
2 spring onions
pinch of sugar
1 bay leaf
seasoning
water
cornflour or arrowroot

Joint the pheasants into legs and breasts. Peel and de-seed the papaya and cut lengthwise into 8 portions.

Place the pheasants in a heavy-bottomed pan with a little water. Season, then cover the pan with a tight-fitting lid and bring slowly to the boil. Simmer gently for 15 minutes, or until the pheasant is nearly cooked.

Add the orange and lemon juices, and the papaya. Replace the lid and cook for a few minutes longer until the pheasant is tender. Remove the pheasant and place it on a serving dish. Decorate each piece with a slice of papaya.

Correct the seasoning of the pan juices, adding a pinch of sugar. Thicken with a little arrowroot or cornflour mixed with water. Strain over the pheasant and serve.

Roast Pheasant with Mushroom and Chestnut Stuffing

TIME TO ALLOW: 1½ hours
SERVES 4-5

1 pheasant, about 3-4 pounds (1.5-2 kg)
8 ounces (200 g) can unsweetened chestnut purée
4 ounces (100 g) button mushrooms, washed and chopped finely
⅛ pint (75 ml) cream
1 egg
3 rashers of fatty bacon
oil
seasoning
flour
1 pint (600 ml) vegetable stock or water

Mix the chestnut purée, mushrooms, cream and egg lightly together and season. Place the mixture inside the pheasant and rub with oil and seasoning. Cover with bacon rashers.

Place the pheasant in a roasting dish with a little water in the bottom and roast in a moderately hot oven (375°F/190°C/gas regulo 4-5) until slightly underdone (about 45-55 minutes). Remove the pheasant from the roasting dish and keep warm.

With such a delightful stuffing a plain roast gravy is most suitable with this dish. Add 3 ounces (75 g) flour to the residue in the roasting pan, mix to a smooth paste then add hot water or vegetable stock. Mix thoroughly then bring to the boil, season and simmer for a few minutes.

Roast pheasant is at its best slightly underdone because it remains moist.

VARIATION
Cold leftovers of roast pheasant with mushroom and chestnut stuffing make a delicious and unusual dish for afternoon tea.

Slice a loaf of french bread on an angle, butter lightly and spread with a layer of mushroom and chestnut stuffing.

Slice the pheasant thinly and place a generous amount on each piece of bread.

Decorate to taste.

Pheasant Sauté Calvados

TIME TO ALLOW: 45 minutes
SERVES 6 to 8

2 pheasants, each about 1½ pounds (650 g)
2 large apples
¼ pint (150 ml) Calvados (apple liqueur)
juice from 1 lemon
½ pint (300 ml) cream
oil
flour
seasoning

Joint the pheasants into breasts and legs, dust with flour and brown in oil in a heavy-bottomed frying pan. Season, then remove the pheasant pieces and keep warm.

Peel and core the apples and slice them into neat segments. Place the apples in the pan, pour over the Calvados and lemon, and bring to the boil. Return the pheasant to the pan, cover the pan with a lid or foil and allow to simmer gently until cooked, about 15 minutes.

Remove the pheasant from the pan and dress on a serving dish. Keep warm. Add the cream to the pan, bring to the boil and correct the seasoning. Reduce the volume of the sauce by a quarter with gentle simmering, then pour over the pheasant before serving.

Pheasant Sauté with Vermouth

TIME TO ALLOW: 45 minutes
SERVES 6-8

2 pheasants, each about 2 pounds (1 kg)
1 medium onion, chopped finely
1 capsicum, sliced thinly
8 ounces (200 g) bacon rashers, cut into slices
½ pint (300 ml) dry vermouth
¼ pint (150 ml) cream
flour
oil
seasoning

Joint the pheasants into legs and breasts and dust with flour. Heat a heavy-bottomed frying pan and brown the pheasants in oil. Season, then remove from the pan and keep warm.

Place the onions, capsicum and bacon in the pan and sauté on a low heat until tender. Add the vermouth and replace the pheasant. Cover and simmer until tender (about 20-25 minutes).

Place the pheasant on a serving tray and keep warm. Add the cream to the sauce and taste to correct the seasoning. Pour the sauce over the pheasant and serve.

Barbecued Pheasant

TIME TO ALLOW: 45 minutes
SERVES 4 to 6

2 pheasant, each about 2 pounds (1 kg)
¼ pint (150 ml) spicy barbecue sauce
¼ pint (150 ml) oil
juice from 1 lemon
1 clove garlic, crushed

Mix together the barbecue sauce, oil, lemon juice and garlic. Halve the pheasants and rub with the barbecue mixture and leave to marinate for 10-15 minutes.

When the barbecue is hot, cook the pheasant halves, browning on both sides and cooking for 15-20 minutes. Serve.

Should you want to prepare this recipe without a barbecue, heat the oven on grill with the thermostat on full. Grill the pheasants in a roasting tray directly below the element until cooked.

Pheasant Casserole

TIME TO ALLOW: 45 minutes
SERVES 6 to 8

2 pheasants, each about 2 pounds (1 kg)
2 ounces (50 g) butter
1 medium onion, chopped finely
2 bacon rashers with rind removed, chopped finely
1 clove garlic, crushed
¼ pint (150 ml) white wine
¾ pint (450 ml) hot stock or water
1 bay leaf
flour
seasoning

Joint the pheasants into legs and breasts, and dust with flour. Melt the butter in a heavy-bottomed casserole. Brown the onions in the butter and add the pheasant portions. Brown the pheasant on both sides, season, and add the diced bacon and the garlic. Cook for a few minutes, then add the wine and just enough stock (or water) to cover. Add the bay leaf and bring to the boil. Simmer gently for 20-25 minutes, or until the pheasant is tender. Correct the seasoning.

Serve with rice or creamed potatoes.

Pheasant with Sauerkraut

This dish is suitable for cooking older birds.

TIME TO ALLOW: 2¼ hours
SERVES 6

1 pheasant, about 3-4 pounds (1.5-2 kg)
1½ pounds (750 g) sauerkraut
8 ounces (200 g) smoked sausages (frankfurters)
4 ounces (100 g) streaky bacon
1 large onion, chopped
seasoning
pinch of caraway seeds
oil

Place half the sauerkraut in a large casserole. Meanwhile brown the pheasant in hot oil in a heavy-bottomed frying pan. When the pheasant is evenly browned, place it in the casserole on top of the sauerkraut.

Fry the onion in the pan from which the pheasant has been taken, then add it to the casserole. Cover the pheasant with the bacon rashers, and skin and slice the frankfurters and place them around the pheasant. Sprinkle with seasoning and a pinch of caraway seeds. Surround the pheasant with the balance of the sauerkraut.

Cover the casserole and cook in a moderate oven (375°F/190°C/gas regulo 4-5) for 2 hours or until the pheasant is tender.

Braised Pheasant with Madeira

TIME TO ALLOW: 1½ hours
SERVES 4

1 pheasant, about 3-4 pounds (1.5-2 kg)
4 ounces (100 g) fatty bacon, diced
2 ounces (50 g) ham, diced
1 medium onion, chopped finely
1 stick of celery, chopped finely
1 clove of garlic, crushed
1 small bunch of parsley, chopped
1 ounce (25 g) butter
pinch of freshly ground nutmeg
seasoning
¼ pint (150 ml) Madeira
½ pint (300 ml) water

Place the pheasant in a large casserole or stew-pan and add all the other ingredients and seasoning, except for the Madeira and the water.

Cook on a moderate heat (375°F/190°C/gas regulo 4-5) until the pheasant begins to brown, then add the Madeira and water. Cover and allow to finish cooking about 1 hour.

Remove the pheasant and place on a serving dish. Strain the fat from the sauce and pass the vegetables through a sieve. Pour the sauce over the pheasant and serve.

Pheasant Pie

TIME TO ALLOW: 1 hour
SERVES 4

1 pheasant about 2 pounds (1 kg)
1 medium onion, chopped finely
4 ounces (100 g) ham, diced
2 ounces (50 g) mushrooms, washed and chopped
½ pint (300 ml) stock or water
8 ounces (200 g) puff pastry
a beaten egg
oil
pinch of cayenne pepper
seasoning

Strip the meat from the pheasant and cut into small pieces.

Heat a frying pan and fry the onion in oil until soft. Add the pheasant meat, ham, and mushrooms, then season. Add just enough stock to cover the pheasant, bring to the boil and simmer for a few minutes. Pour the mixture into a pie dish and cover with a thin layer of pastry. Make a small hole in the centre of the pastry, then brush pastry with the beaten egg. Bake in a moderate oven (375°F/190°C/gas regulo 4-5) for 20-30 minutes when it will be a beautiful golden brown.

Pheasant in Tortilla

TIME TO ALLOW: 30 minutes
SERVES 6

2 pounds (1 kg) cooked pheasant, chopped
1 medium onion, chopped
1 clove garlic, crushed
oil
1 tomato, chopped
¼ pint (150 ml) chilli sauce
¼ pint (150 ml) red wine
seasoning
6 tortilla shells
8 ounces (200 g) grated cheese

Sauté the pheasant, onion and garlic in oil in a hot frying pan. Add the tomato, chilli sauce and seasoning to taste. Cook for 3-4 minutes, then add the wine. Cover and simmer for a further 2-3 minutes.

Place the mixture in tortillas on a baking dish, cover with grated cheese and bake in a moderate oven (375°F/190°C/gas regulo 4-5) for 20-25 minutes.

Spicy Pheasant Salad

TIME TO ALLOW: 30 minutes
SERVES 8

2 pounds (1 kg) cooked pheasant
1 medium onion, sliced finely
8 ounces (200 g) courgettes, sliced thinly on an angle
1 fresh chilli, de-seeded and chopped finely
3 medium tomatoes, segmented
1 clove garlic, crushed
⅛ pint (75 ml) white vinegar
¼ pint (150 ml) oil
⅛ pint (75 ml) cold water
⅛ pint (75 ml) chilli sauce

Blend the pheasant and vegetables and toss lightly. Add the oil, vinegar, water and chilli sauce and taste to correct the seasoning.

This is an unusual addition to a buffet table or a delicious cold luncheon dish.

Pheasant Salad

TIME TO ALLOW: 30 minutes
SERVES 8 entrées

2 pounds (1 kg) cooked pheasant, cut into matchsticks
6 ounces (150 g) celery, cut into thin strips across the grain
3 sharp apples, peeled, cored and cut into matchsticks
1 ounce (25 g) sunflower seeds, toasted
¼ pint (150 ml) pineapple juice
½ pint (300 ml) prepared mayonnaise

Blend the pheasant, celery, apples and sunflower seeds and toss lightly. Add the pineapple juice and the mayonnaise and season to taste.

Dress on butterhead lettuce leaves and decorate with a sprinkling of toasted sunflower seeds, a rosette of tomato and a sprig of mint.

146

QUAIL

HUNTING SEASON
This bird is protected in the wild and is farmed for the table.

Quails must be eaten really fresh, preferably twenty-four hours after being killed. They should be plucked as soon as possible after being killed. Quail do not need to be hung and, if they are, they should never be allowed to get too 'high'.

Quail are such small birds, that, unlike most game, they can be cooked relatively quickly. They may be split and flattened and cooked under a grill, but they will benefit from marinating beforehand and should be well basted throughout.

Quail Soup with Green Beans

TIME TO ALLOW: 30 minutes (or 2½ hours including preparation of stock)
SERVES 6

2 quail
2 pints (1200 ml) good stock
2 ounces (50 g) butter
2 ounces (50 g) flour
8 ounces (200 g) fresh green beans
pinch of savory, chopped
seasoning

Boil the quail in the prepared stock for 10-15 minutes. Remove the quail and reserve the stock.

Melt the butter in a heavy-bottomed saucepan and add the flour. Cook for a few minutes, cool slightly, then add the hot stock. Stir continuously to avoid lumps, and bring slowly to the boil. Season to taste.

Meanwhile, string the beans and plunge them into boiling water. Return the water to the boil, then remove the beans and chill in cold water. Slice on an angle and add to the soup.

Bone the quail and slice the meat neatly and add to the soup. Add the savory, simmer for a few minutes, then taste to correct the seasoning before serving.

Chilled Quail Soup with Pecan Nuts

TIME TO ALLOW: 30 minutes (or 2½ hours if making the stock)
SERVES 6

2 quail
2 pints (1200 ml) good stock
12 ounces (300 g) pecan nuts, ground finely
seasoning
a little whipped cream (with no sugar)

Boil the quail in the prepared stock for 10-15 minutes, remove, and take the meat from the bones. Add the quail meat and ground pecan nuts to the stock and pass through a blender, mixing thoroughly. Allow the soup to cool, then check the seasoning.

Serve with a rosette of whipped cream piped neatly in each bowl.

This is a delicious and very easy soup to prepare with a stock made from the bones and scraps of a previous roast quail dinner.

Quail with Lettuce

TIME TO ALLOW: 30 minutes
SERVES 4

8 quail
4 ounces (100 g) fatty bacon
2 lettuces
2 apples, peeled, cored and quartered
¾ pint (450 ml) stock or water
seasoning

Remove the cores from the lettuces then plunge each lettuce into boiling water. Return the water to the boil, then drain, and rinse the lettuce under cold water. Squeeze out the remaining water, slice neatly, and spread the lettuce over the bottom of a deep roasting dish.

Clean the quail, put a quarter apple in each, and place them on top of the lettuce. Drape a slice of fatty bacon over each quail, and pour in the stock. Season and place in a moderately hot oven (400°F/205°C/gas regulo 6) for 15 minutes.

Remove the quail to a serving dish and keep warm. Taste the lettuce sauce to correct the seasoning, and pour over the quail to serve.

Casseroled Quail with Vegetables

TIME TO ALLOW: 30 minutes
SERVES 4

8 quail
¼ pint (150 ml) white wine
⅛ pint (75 ml) brandy
½ pint (300 ml) stock or water
1 medium onion
2 stalks celery
2 carrots
1 leek

Flour the quail, then brown them in oil in a heavy-bottomed casserole. Slice the vegetables very thinly, add them to the casserole and cook for a few minutes.

Drain off the fat, add the brandy and set alight. When the flames die down add the wine and stock. Season lightly, cover, and place in a moderately hot oven (400°F/205°C/gas regulo 6) for 10 minutes. Check the sauce to correct the seasoning and cook for a further 2-3 minutes.

Serve the quail with the vegetable sauce poured over them.

Quail with Braised Rice

TIME TO ALLOW: 30 minutes
SERVES 4

8 quail
2 small onions, diced finely
3 ounces (75 g) bacon
6 ounces (150 g) rice
1 ounce (25 g) butter
1 capsicum, seeded
1 pint (600 ml) stock or water
2 spring onions

Melt the butter in a heavy-bottomed saucepan, then add the onions, diced bacon and diced capsicum. Fry for 2-3 minutes, then add the stock, quail and rice. Season, then stir until boiling and simmer for 7-8 minutes. Remove the quail and keep warm.

Continue to simmer the rice until it is nearly cooked, by which time most of the stock will have been absorbed. Transfer the rice to a baking dish and place the quail on top of it. Bake in a moderate oven (375°F/190°C/gas regulo 4-5) for a further 10-12 minutes, until the rice is cooked and the quail are tender.

Place the quail on a serving dish and keep hot. Finely slice the spring onions and add to the rice. Taste to correct the seasoning and surround the quails with a ring of braised rice to serve.

Quail with Ham Stuffing

TIME TO ALLOW: 1 hour
SERVES 4

8 quail
8 ounces (200 g) cooked ham, diced
4 ounces (100 g) fresh white breadcrumbs
2 cloves garlic, crushed
1 small bunch Italian parsley, chopped finely. (Use ordinary parsley if the
   stronger Italian parsley is unavailable.)
1 egg, beaten lightly
1 ounce (25 g) butter
½ pint (300 ml) stock or water
1 ounce (25 g) tomato paste
oil
seasoning

Combine the ham, breadcrumbs, garlic and parsley, mixing lightly. Season
to taste and add the beaten egg. Divide the mixture evenly and place inside
the quail.

Heat a heavy-bottomed casserole and melt the butter, adding a little oil.
When hot, brown the quail evenly. Mix the stock with the tomato paste
and pour over the quail. Cover the casserole and simmer gently in a
moderate oven (375°F/190°C/gas regulo 4-5) for 20 minutes, or until the
quail are tender. Taste to correct the seasoning. Serve the quail on a bed
of rice.

Quail with Toasted Almonds

TIME TO ALLOW: 30 minutes
SERVES 4

8 quail
flour
oil
seasoning
½ pint (300 ml) white wine
6 ounces (150 g) blanched, slivered almonds
¼ pint (150 ml) cream

Clean the quail, dust with flour, then season. Heat a heavy-bottomed casserole, add the oil, and fry the quail until evenly browned. Add the wine, cover, and bake in a moderate oven (375°F/190°C/gas regulo 4-5) for 10 minutes.

Meanwhile toast the almonds in the oven until golden. Add the almonds and cream to the quail, taste to correct the seasoning, and return to the oven for a further 10 minutes, or until the quail are tender.

Arrange the quail on a serving dish and serve the sauce separately.

Steamed Quail with Rosemary

TIME TO ALLOW: 45 minutes
SERVES 4

8 quail
2 sprigs fresh rosemary (each about 6 inches (15 cm))
½ pint (300 ml) white wine
1 pint (600 ml) stock or water
1 medium onion, sliced thinly
6 black peppercorns
1 bay leaf
1 clove garlic, peeled and squashed (but intact)
1 ounce (25 g) arrowroot or cornflour, mixed with cold water

Choose a large steamer or a large, deep casserole (preferably stainless steel) with a tight-fitting lid. It should be large enough for a wire rack to sit inside.

Strip the leaves off the rosemary stalks, placing 3 or 4 inside each quail and saving the rest for the sauce. Put the wine, stock, onion, bay leaf, garlic, peppercorns and rosemary stalks in the casserole and bring to the boil. Simmer for 15 minutes until the volume has been reduced by about a quarter.

Put a wire rack into the casserole dish so it is just clear of the stock. Place the quail on the wire rack, season, and cover the dish with a tight-fitting lid and steam for 12 minutes, or until the quail are tender. Place the quail on a serving dish and keep warm.

Thicken the stock with the cornflour or arrowroot, bring to the boil and correct the seasoning. Strain the sauce into a clean pot and add the remaining rosemary leaves. Return to the boil, then pour over the quail before serving.

Quail with Mayonnaise

TIME TO ALLOW: 1 hour, plus ½ hour to chill quail

8 quail, roasted
½ pint (300 ml) prepared mayonnaise
various salads

The ideal light luncheon. Serve seasonal salads (potato, slaw, fresh bean, tomato, etc.) with freshly roasted, chilled quail. Serve simply with the mayonnaise. Try adding chopped, fresh tarragon to the mayonnaise for an extra lift.

PIGEON

HUNTING SEASON
Any time

Pigeon should be eaten as squabs, or young birds, when they have pale pink flesh. The flesh darkens with age to a dark red colour and a bird like this will be rather tough even after long slow cooking.

Pigeons are not usually hung. It is customary to leave the liver inside the bird when dressing it.

Pigeon Soup

Ideal for pigeons that do not have youth on their side

TIME TO ALLOW: 3 hours
SERVES 6

2 pigeons
2 pints (1200 ml) water
8 ounces (200 g) vegetables (carrot, onion, celery, leek)
1 bay leaf
6 peppercorns
2 ounces (50 g) butter
2 ounces (50 g) flour
¼ pint (150 ml) cream
parsley, chopped

Add the cold water to the pigeons in a large pot, bring to the boil, then skim any scum which appears. Add the vegetables, bay leaf and peppercorns, and simmer slowly for 2 hours, topping up with cold water as necessary. Strain the stock and remove and dice the pigeon meat, reserving for the soup.

Melt the butter in a heavy-bottomed saucepan, then add the flour and cook for a few minutes. Cool slightly before adding the hot stock, stirring to avoid lumps. Season and bring to the boil, then simmer for 15-20 minutes before adding the pigeon meat. Taste to correct the seasoning and heat through thoroughly.

Serve with a dash of whipped cream sprinkled with a garnish of chopped parsley.

Roast Pigeon with Asparagus Sauce

TIME TO ALLOW: 2½ hours
SERVES 4

4 pigeons
1 pint (600 ml) hot stock or water
¼ pint (150 ml) cream
4 ounces (100 g) fresh asparagus (green or white)
2 ounces (50 g) flour
oil
seasoning

Leaving the livers in the pigeons, season the birds and rub with oil, then place in a roasting tray. Roast in a moderate oven (375°F/190°C/gas regulo 4-5) for 1½-2 hours, or until tender. Remove pigeons from roasting dish and keep warm.

Meanwhile, peel the stalks of the asparagus, plunge them into rapidly boiling water, return to the boil, then remove and cool in cold water. Slice the blanched asparagus into neat slices on an angle, and set aside.

Sprinkle the flour into the pan juices and mix to a smooth paste. Add stock and cook for a few minutes, stirring constantly. Season, then bring to the boil. Strain into a clean saucepan, add the asparagus and simmer gently until it is tender. Taste to correct the seasoning.

Pour some of the sauce over the pigeons on a serving dish, keeping the balance in a sauceboat.

Roast Pigeon with Apple and Sauerkraut Stuffing

TIME TO ALLOW: 2½ hours
SERVES 4

4 pigeons
6 ounces (150 g) fatty bacon, chopped
1 large onion, chopped finely
2 apples, peeled, cored and diced
1 ounce (25 g) brown sugar
1 pound (450 g) sauerkraut
pinch each of thyme and caraway seeds
oil
seasoning

Fry the onion and bacon in a heavy-bottomed frying pan in a little oil until the onions are transparent. Add the apples, brown sugar, caraway seeds and thyme and continue to fry for a further 5 minutes. Drain the sauerkraut and add to the pan. Mix all the ingredients and taste to correct the seasoning.

Place this stuffing inside the pigeons, season and rub them with oil. Place the pigeons in a roasting tray and roast in a moderate oven (375°F/190°C/gas regulo 4-5) for 1½-2 hours, or until tender.

Add a few slices of gherkin to a plain roast gravy for a complementary sauce.

Roast Pigeon with Bacon Sauce

TIME TO ALLOW: 2½ hours
SERVES 4

4 pigeons
4 ounces (100 g) streaky bacon, cut into strips
1 medium onion, shredded
juice and zest from half a lemon
½ pint (300 ml) stock or water
1 ounce (25 g) flour
seasoning
oil

Clean the pigeons, leaving the livers inside. Season, rub with oil, and place in a roasting tray. Pour in the stock, then cover with foil and roast in a moderate oven (375°F/190°C/gas regulo 4-5) for 2 hours, or until tender. Remove to a serving tray and keep warm.

Heat a little oil in a heavy-bottomed saucepan and fry the onions until transparent. Add the bacon, then the lemon zest and juice. Mix in the flour to a smooth paste then strain the hot stock from the roasting tray into the mixture, stirring constantly until it thickens as it comes to the boil. If too thick, add a little stock or water. Taste to correct the seasoning. Coat the pigeons with the sauce and serve.

Roast Pigeon with Liver and Anchovy Stuffing

TIME TO ALLOW: 2½ hours
SERVES 4

4 pigeons
1 medium onion, chopped finely
1 clove garlic, crushed
8 ounces (200 g) pigeon and chicken livers
1 ounce (25 g) anchovy fillets, pounded to a paste
2 slices fresh white bread, diced
1 egg
1 pint (600 ml) stock or water
1 ounce (25 g) flour
oil
seasoning

Pan-fry the onions in a little oil until transparent, add the garlic and fry a little longer, then add the diced livers, pounded anchovies and diced bread. Allow to cool slightly then add the lightly beaten egg. Season, then divide the stuffing evenly and place inside the pigeons.

Put the pigeons in a roasting tray, rub with oil and season. Cover with foil and roast in a moderate oven (375°F/190°C/gas regulo 4-5) for 2 hours, or until tender. Remove to a serving tray and keep warm.

Mix the flour to a smooth paste with the roasting tray juices, cook for a few minutes, then stir in the hot stock. Bring to the boil, season, and simmer for a few minutes. Taste to correct the seasoning, then strain over the pigeons.

Roast Pigeon with Raisin Stuffing

TIME TO ALLOW: 2½ hours
SERVES 4

4 pigeons
½ pint (300 ml) milk
4 slices fresh white bread
8 ounces (200 g) seedless raisins
¼ pint (105 ml) stock
oil
seasoning

Soak the bread in the milk, then squeeze off any excess milk. Soak the raisins in the stock until tender and soft, then drain. Mix the raisins and bread together and season lightly. Spoon the stuffing into the pigeons and place them in a roasting tray. Rub with oil and season. Cook in a hot oven (425°F/220°C/gas regulo 7) for 1½-2 hours. When tender, transfer to a serving dish.

A simple roast gravy made from the pan-juices is best with this dish.

Braised Pigeon with Cheese and Green Peppercorn Stuffing

TIME TO ALLOW: 2½ hours
SERVES 4

4 pigeons
8 ounces (200 g) cheese
1 ounce (25 g) green peppercorns
½ ounce (12 g) prepared French mustard
1 egg yolk
⅛ pint (75 ml) beer or lager
2 ounces (50 g) flour
1 pint (600 ml) hot stock or water
oil
seasoning

Grate the cheese and mix with the peppercorns, mustard and egg yolk. Blend thoroughly, then add a little beer, taking care not to make the mixture too wet.

Divide the stuffing equally between the pigeons and place inside. Season the birds and rub with oil. Place them in a roasting tray and roast in a moderate oven (375°F/190°C/gas regulo 4-5) for about 1½ hours. Remove the pigeons from the roasting tray and keep warm.

Mix the flour with the roasting tray residue to a smooth paste. Cook for a few minutes, allow to cool slightly, then stir in the hot stock. Bring to the boil. Season, and simmer for a few minutes. Taste to correct the seasoning, then return the pigeons to the sauce and braise for 45-60 minutes in a moderate oven.

To serve, arrange in a serving dish and spoon the sauce over the pigeons.

Braised Pigeon with Fresh Herbs

TIME TO ALLOW: 2½ hours
SERVES 4

4 pigeons
2 ounces (50 g) flour
1 pint (600 ml) hot stock or water
6 ounces (150 g) fresh herbs (tarragon, basil, marjoram)
1 clove garlic, crushed
1 medium onion, chopped finely
1 bay leaf
oil
salt
freshly ground black pepper

Heat a heavy-bottomed casserole (or deep roasting tray) and fry the onions and garlic in oil. Dust the pigeons with flour and add to the casserole, browning evenly. Season with salt and freshly ground black pepper.

Add the stock, half the herbs and the bay leaf. Cover with foil and braise in a moderate oven (375°F/190°C/gas regulo 4-5) for 1½-2 hours, or until tender. Remove the pigeons to a serving tray and keep warm.

Strain the sauce into a clean saucepan and correct the seasoning. Bring to the boil and add the remainder of the chopped herbs. Pour sauce over the pigeons to serve.

Roast Pigeon with Pistachio Stuffing

TIME TO ALLOW: 2 hours
SERVES 4

4 dove pigeons
1 medium onion, chopped finely
2 rashers bacon, chopped finely
liver and kidney from pigeons, chopped finely
6 ounces (150 g) shelled pistachio nuts, chopped
6 ounces (150 g) fresh white breadcrumbs
1/8 pint (75 ml) milk
1/8 pint (75 ml) Amaretto (almond liqueur)
1 egg
oil
seasoning

Fry the onion in a heavy-bottomed frying pan in a little oil, then add the bacon and offal and continue to fry for a few minutes. Allow to cool slightly before adding the pistachio nuts and breadcrumbs. Mix lightly, then add the milk and beaten egg, seasoning, and lastly the liqueur. Divide the mixture evenly and place inside the pigeons.

Season the pigeons and rub with oil, and place in a roasting tray with a little water. Cover with tinfoil and roast in a moderately hot oven (375°F/190°C/gas regulo 4-5) for 1½ hours, or until tender. (Not all pigeons will be ready together, some may take 2 hours or longer). When tender remove foil, brush with a little oil, and allow to brown.

Serve a roast gravy flavoured with Marsala as a complementary sauce.

Roast pigeon with pistachio stuffing

Boiled Pigeon with Pease Pudding

TIME TO ALLOW: 4½ hours (after soaking peas)
SERVES 4

4 pigeons
4 carrots, peeled
2 onions, stuck with 4 cloves each
2 small leeks, washed and trimmed
4 parsnips, peeled
8 ounces (200 g) salt pork

Place all the ingredients in a large saucepan, cover with cold water and bring to the boil. Skim, then simmer until the vegetables are tender. Remove the vegetables and salt pork and set aside, but continue to simmer the pigeons until they are tender, about 1½-2 hours.

Remove the pigeons and place them on a serving tray. Surround with the re-heated vegetables sprinkled with the chopped salt pork, and serve with the pease pudding.

PEASE PUDDING
1 pound (450 g) split peas
1 medium onion, sliced thinly
4 ounces (100 g) butter
3 eggs, beaten
salt
freshly ground black pepper
grated nutmeg

Soak the peas in cold water overnight. Drain and place in a saucepan with the onion, cover with water, bring to the boil, and simmer for 2-4 hours, or until peas are cooked. Purée the peas through a moulie or sieve.

Combine the peas, butter and eggs and season with salt, black pepper and nutmeg. Mix well and place in a buttered pudding basin. Place the basin in a tray of water and bake in a moderate oven (375°F/190°C/gas regulo 4-5) until done, about 30-45 minutes. Alternatively, the mixture can be placed in a scalded, buttered and floured cloth, tied up, and cooked with the pigeons.

Pigeon and Apple Salad

TIME TO ALLOW: 2 hours for roasting, 15 minutes for salad preparation
SERVES 8 entrées, or 4 main courses

4 pigeons
4 crisp apples, peeled and cored
small bunch of chives, cut into short lengths
juice from 1 lemon
½ pint (300 ml) prepared mayonnaise
seasoning
oil

Season the pigeons and rub with oil and place them in a roasting tray with a little water. Roast in a moderate oven (375°F/190°C/gas regulo 4-5) for 1½-2 hours, or until tender. Remove the pigeons from the oven and when cool, joint them, remove the bones and slice the meat.

Cut the apples into neat segments and combine with the pigeon meat. Season lightly and add the lemon juice and chives and blend lightly with the mayonnaise.

This salad is suitable as a luncheon dish or as a light entrée for a formal dinner.

GUINEA FOWL

HUNTING SEASON
Once a game bird, guinea fowl are now reared for the table all year round.

Guinea fowl flesh has a flavour half-way between pheasant and chicken. It is at its best when the fowl weighs about 700-900 g (1½-2 lb). If you buy a freshly killed bird, choose one with a plump breast and smooth legs. Hang, head downwards, for a couple of days in a cool, airy place, before gutting.

Roast Guinea Fowl with Mushrooms

TIME TO ALLOW: 1 hour
SERVES 6

2 plump guinea fowl
1 ounce (25 g) flour
¾ pint (450 ml) hot stock or water
¼ pint (150 ml) Madeira
1 medium onion, chopped finely
12 ounces (300 g) mushrooms, washed and sliced
oil
seasoning

Season the guinea fowl and rub with oil. Roast in a moderate oven (375°F/190°C/gas regulo 4-5) for 45 minutes. Remove the guinea fowl to a serving dish and keep warm.

Add the flour to the roasting tray juices and mix to a smooth paste. Cook for a few minutes, then add the hot stock and Madeira. Bring to the boil and season. Strain into a clean saucepan and add the onions and mushrooms. Cook until the onions are tender. Taste to correct the seasoning, then spoon the sauce over the guinea fowl.

Serve with creamed potatoes, artichoke bottoms filled with green peas, and cauliflower with hollandaise sauce.

Spicy Roast Guinea Fowl

TIME TO ALLOW: 1 hour
SERVES 4 to 6

2 plump guinea fowl
½ teaspoon each of the following:
    chilli powder, cumin seeds, coriander seeds, chopped coriander leaves
juice from 1 orange
juice from 1 lemon
2 cloves garlic, crushed
salt
freshly ground pepper
¼ pint (150 ml) oil

1 ounce (25 g) flour
1 pint (600 ml) hot stock or water

Mix all the ingredients (except for flour and stock) to a paste and rub over the guinea fowl. Leave to stand overnight, or for as long as possible to allow the flavours to be absorbed.

Place the guinea fowl in a roasting dish and roast in a moderate oven (375°F/190°C/gas regulo 4-5) for 45 minutes, then remove to a serving dish and keep warm.

Blend the flour to a smooth paste with the roasting tray juices, cook a few minutes, then add the hot stock, stirring all the time until it comes to the boil. Season. Simmer for a few minutes, taste the sauce to correct the seasoning then strain over the guinea fowl.

Serve with game chips (gaufrettes), glazed button onions, and braised lettuce.

Sautéed Guinea Fowl with Green Pepper and Tomato

TIME TO ALLOW: 45 minutes
SERVES 6

3 young guinea fowl
2 medium onions, peeled and sliced
1 clove garlic, crushed
2 green peppers, seeded and sliced
3 medium tomatoes, sliced
2 leaves fresh basil
flour
oil
seasoning

Cut each guinea fowl into two legs and two breasts and dust with flour. Brown in oil in a heavy-bottomed frying pan. Remove the birds and keep warm.

Sauté the onion and garlic until clear then add the green pepper, tomatoes and basil and return the guinea fowl to the pan. Season, and cover the pan with a lid. Cook until tender, about 20-25 minutes. Serve on a bed of rice flavoured with saffron.

Sautéed Guinea Fowl in Champagne

TIME TO ALLOW: 45 minutes
SERVES 6

3 young guinea fowl
6 ounces (150 g) butter
½ pint (300 ml) dry champagne
seasoning

Cut each guinea fowl into two legs and two breasts and sauté quickly in butter. Season, then cover and cook slowly for 15-20 minutes. Remove the guinea fowl to a serving dish and keep warm.

Add the champagne to the pan juices, bring to the boil and simmer until a smooth consistency is reached. Strain the sauce over the guinea fowl and serve.

Such a delicate dish should be accompanied with mild-flavoured, simply prepared seasonal vegetables.

Braised Guinea Fowl with Grain Mustard

TIME TO ALLOW: 1 hour
SERVES 4-6

2 or 3 guinea fowl
1 clove garlic, crushed
2 tablespoons grain mustard
¼ pint (150 ml) white wine
flour
oil
seasoning

Cut each guinea fowl into two legs and two breasts and dust with flour. Heat a heavy-bottomed frying pan with a little oil and brown the guinea fowl. Season, then lower heat and continue to cook for 10-15 minutes.

Stir in the garlic and grain mustard, cook for a few minutes, then add the wine. Bring to the boil, cover, and simmer for about 15 minutes or until the guinea fowl are tender. Taste to correct seasoning.

Serve with sauce spooned over.

Casseroled Guinea Fowl with Prawns

TIME TO ALLOW: 1 hour
SERVES 6

2 or 3 guinea fowl
1 large onion, peeled and sliced
1 clove garlic, crushed
1 pint (600 ml) hot stock or water
1 bay leaf
1 large carrot, peeled and sliced
4 ounces (100 g) celeriac, peeled and diced
1 pound (450 g) potatoes, peeled and diced
12 raw prawns, peeled and de-veined
1 ounce (25 g) cornflour, mixed with a little water
oil
seasoning

Place the onions and garlic in a casserole dish with a little oil. Cook in a moderate oven (375°F/190°C/gas regulo 4-5) for 5 minutes. Add the guinea fowl and season. Cover with the stock and add the bay leaf. Place a lid on the casserole and continue cooking in a moderate oven for 20 minutes.

Add the carrots, celeriac and potatoes and cook for a further 15 minutes. Add the prawns and cook until the prawns are lightly done, about 5 minutes. Taste to correct seasoning, then thicken with cornflour.

This is a meal in itself and requires no other garnish.

Guinea Fowl Salad with Pickled Walnuts

TIME TO ALLOW: 30 minutes
SERVES 6 entrées

1½ pounds (650 g) guinea fowl, cooked and boned
1 medium onion, sliced
2 medium tomatoes, cut into wedges
¼ pint (150 ml) white vinegar
⅛ pint (75 ml) cold water
⅛ pint (75 ml) walnut oil
6 ounces (150 g) pickled walnuts, halved
½ pint (300 ml) oil
Seasoning

Slice the guinea fowl and combine with the onion and tomatoes in a large bowl. Season lightly, then add the vinegar, water and walnut oil. Blend lightly. Add the pickled walnuts and oil. Toss gently and taste to correct seasoning.
    Serve as an appetiser or as a main dish in its own right.

Guinea Fowl and Kiwifruit Salad

TIME TO ALLOW: 30 minutes
SERVES 6 entrées

1½ pounds (650 g) guinea fowl, cooked and boned
1 red pepper, de-seeded and sliced
6 kiwifruit, peeled and sliced
8 ounces (200 g) plain yoghurt
Seasoning

Slice the guinea fowl and combine with the red pepper and kiwifruit in a large bowl. Season lightly. Add the yoghurt and blend carefully, taking care not to break the kiwifruit slices.

PARTRIDGE

HUNTING SEASON
1st September–1st February

Partridges should be hung by their necks in a cool airy place, young birds for three to four days, older ones for a week. The common grey partridge is often thought to be finer in texture and taste than the red-leg partridge.

Partridge and quail belong to the same family as pheasants. Young birds can be distinguished by their flexible beaks and pointed rather than rounded outside flight feathers.

Steamed Partridge with Pineapple

TIME TO ALLOW: 1 hour
SERVES 6

6 partridge (young birds are best suited to this recipe)
6 large or 12 small slices pineapple
6 bacon rashers
1 pint (600 ml) stock or water
¼ pint (150 ml) pineapple juice

Wrap the bacon rashers around the partridges and place them in an ovenproof dish. Add the stock and pineapple juice. Surround with the pineapple slices and cover the dish with a tight-fitting lid. Cook in a moderately hot oven (400°F/205°C/gas regulo 6) for 30-45 minutes, or until tender.

The sauce may be lightly thickened with a little cornflour mixed with cold water if preferred.

Although not strictly steaming, this method gives the qualities of steaming and retains the cooking liquor for use in the sauce.

Partridge Casserole

TIME TO ALLOW: 2½ to 3 hours
SERVES 6

3 large partridge (older birds are suitable for this recipe)
¼ pint (150 ml) oil
1 pint (600 ml) white wine
⅛ pine (75 ml) white vinegar
1 large onion, sliced neatly
2 small carrots, sliced neatly
small bunch parsley, chopped
2 cloves garlic, crushed
1 bay leaf
flour
seasoning

Dust the partridges with flour and sauté in oil in a heavy casserole dish. When evenly browned, season and add the wine, vinegar, and bay leaf. Cover the casserole with a lid and braise in a moderate oven (375°F/190°C/gas regulo 4-5) for 1½-2 hours, or until nearly tender.

Add the onions, carrots, garlic and parsley and cook for a further 30 minutes, or until both vegetables and partridge are tender.

Serve from the casserole, spooning vegetables and sauce over the partridge.

Braised Partridge with Sour Cream

TIME TO ALLOW: 1½ to 2 hours
SERVES 6

3 large partridge
1 large onion, diced neatly
1 clove garlic, crushed
6 ounces (150 g) mushrooms, washed and sliced neatly
3 slices fatty bacon
1 pint (600 ml) stock or water
½ pint (300 ml) sour cream
oil
flour
seasoning

Wrap the partridges in the fatty bacon and dust with flour. Brown well in oil in a heavy braising dish, then add the garlic, onion and stock. Cover the dish and braise in a moderate oven (375°F/190°C/gas regulo 4-5) for 1-1¼ hours. Take from the oven, remove the bacon and add the mushrooms and sour cream. Season lightly, then return to the oven and cook for a further ½ hour, or until tender. Taste to correct the seasoning of the sauce.

Carve the partridges and coat with sauce, serving the remainder of the sauce separately.

Roast Partridge with Cabbage

TIME TO ALLOW: 2½ to 3 hours
SERVES 6

6 partridge
1 white cabbage, washed and shredded
1 onion, sliced finely
8 ounces (200 g) fatty bacon, sliced thinly
½ pint (300 ml) stock or water
½ pint (300 ml) white wine
oil
flour
seasoning

Plunge the cabbage into rapidly boiling water, return the water to the boil, then strain.

Dust the partridge with flour and sauté in oil in a heavy-bottomed frying pan until evenly browned. Transfer them to a casserole dish.

Fry the onion and cabbage in a little oil without colouring, season, then arrange around the partridge in the casserole dish. Add the bacon, wine and stock and cover with a lid or foil. Simmer in the oven on a moderate heat (375°F/190°C/gas regulo 4-5) for about one hour. If the partridge are young, they will be tender in this time, but older birds may need up to 2 hours.

Place the partridge on a serving dish and surround them with the drained cabbage to serve.

Sautéed Partridge with Anchovy Sauce

TIME TO ALLOW: 2 hours
SERVES 6

6 young partridge (must be young)
olive oil
2 bay leaves
1 clove garlic, crushed
seasoning

10-12 anchovy fillets, pounded to a paste
4 yolks of hard-boiled eggs
1 clove garlic, crushed
⅛ pint (75 ml) tarragon vinegar
¼ pint (150 ml) olive oil
1 small bunch parsley, washed and chopped finely

Prepare the birds by cutting down one side of the spine, then the other, thus removing the backbone. Open out the partridge so there is a double breast and the legs. Flatten lightly with a cutlet bat or mallet. Marinate in oil with the garlic, bay leaves and freshly ground black pepper, for 1-1¼ hours. Use this time to prepare the sauce.

Heat some oil in a heavy-bottomed pan, then add the anchovies and garlic. Cook slowly for 5 minutes, then add the parsley, vinegar and pounded egg yolks, stirring until well blended. Remove from the heat and allow to cool completely.

Heat the olive oil in a heavy-bottomed frying pan and sauté the partridges on each side until cooked through. Season, then arrange on a heated serving dish and serve the sauce separately.

GROUSE

HUNTING SEASON
Red grouse: 12th August-10th December
Black grouse:20th August-10th December

Young birds have flexible beaks and breastbones, and are at their best between the middle of September and the middle of October.

Grouse should be hung for three to four days, after which they can be grilled whole, if small, or roasted. Some people prefer to eat just the breast of the grouse, rather than the whole bird.

Roast Grouse on Toast

TIME TO ALLOW: 1 hour
SERVES 6

6 young grouse
1 pound (450 g) butter
6 slices fatty bacon
6 slices toast
seasoning
cayenne pepper

Pluck and draw the grouse, reserving the livers. Wipe with a damp cloth and truss ready for roasting. Season the grouse inside and out, and place 1 ounce (25 g) butter inside each bird. Wrap each bird in bacon and brown in a moderately hot oven (400°F/205°C/gas regulo 6). When browned, reduce oven to a moderate heat (375°F/190°C/gas regulo 4-5) and cook until nearly tender, about 30 minutes.

Boil the livers in a little salt water for 10 minutes. When cooked, chop finely (or mince) and mix with the remaining butter. Season with salt and cayenne pepper and a little freshly ground black pepper. Spread this liver mixture on the slices of toast.

Remove the grouse from the oven just before they are cooked through, and halve each one, removing the rib-cage bones. Place each grouse on a slice of toast and return to the oven to finish cooking and to brown the birds, about 10 minutes.

Garnish with watercress and serve with cranberry sauce.

Roast Grouse with Grapes

TIME TO ALLOW: 1 hour
SERVES 6

6 young grouse
½ pint (300 ml) white wine
½ pint (300 ml) stock
⅛ pint (75 ml) cream
1 ounce (25 g) flour
8 ounces (200 g) white grapes, peeled and de-seeded
oil
seasoning

Rub the grouse with oil and season. Place in a roasting tray and roast in a moderate oven (375°F/190°C/gas regulo 4-5) for 45 minutes, or until tender. Remove the grouse and keep warm.

Stir the flour to a smooth paste with the roasting tray juices, cook for a few minutes, then add the hot stock and the wine, stirring all the time to avoid lumps. Simmer for a few minutes, then strain the sauce into a clean saucepan. Add the grapes and return to the boil. Taste to correct the seasoning. Carve the grouse and coat with the sauce to serve.

Roast Grouse with Bread Sauce

TIME TO ALLOW: 1 hour
SERVES 6

6 young grouse
oil
seasoning
1 pint (600 ml) milk
1 large onion, peeled
4 cloves
1 blade mace, or a good pinch of ground nutmeg
4 ounces (100 g) fresh white breadcrumbs
1 ounce (25 g) butter
¼ pint (150 ml) cream
seasoning

Rub the grouse with oil and season. Place in a roasting dish and roast in a moderately hot oven (400°F/205°C/gas regulo 6) for 45 minutes, or until tender.

Meanwhile, heat the milk to just below boiling point in a double boiler, add the onion stuck with the cloves and mace (or nutmeg) and simmer for 30 minutes. Remove the mace and add the breadcrumbs, stirring and beating with a whisk. Season, then add half the butter. Cook slowly, whisking often, then taste to correct the seasoning. Remove the onion, then add the other half of the butter and the cream. Coat the grouse with the sauce to serve.

SNIPE

HUNTING SEASON
12th August-31st January

Snipe are traditionally hung for four days then roasted ungutted, though the gizzards are removed. Many people, however, prefer them to be cooked as soon as possible after they have been caught. They are usually eaten rare. The entrails, known as 'the trail', are eaten and regarded as a great delicacy.

Roast Snipe with Liver Stuffing

TIME TO ALLOW: 45 minutes
SERVES 6

6 snipe
1 medium onion, chopped finely
1 clove garlic, crushed
8 ounces (200 g) fatty bacon, sliced
8 ounces (200 g) chicken and snipe livers, diced
8 ounces (200 g) fresh white bread, diced
¼ pint (150 ml) milk
1 egg, beaten lightly
oil
seasoning

Fry the onion and garlic in a little oil in a heavy-bottomed frying pan. When nearly tender add the bacon and liver and cook for a few minutes. Season to taste. Add the bread, then the milk and egg and mix together lightly. Place stuffing in the snipe, season and rub with oil. Place in roasting tray and roast in a hot oven (400°F/205°C/gas regulo 6) for 10-15 minutes.

Serve with a simple gravy made from the pan juices.

Roast Snipe with Bacon and Hazelnut Sauce

TIME TO ALLOW: 45 minutes
SERVES 6

6 snipe
1 ounce (25 g) butter
1 medium onion, chopped finely
8 ounces (200 g) bacon, chopped finely
1 ounce (25 g) flour
1 pint (600 ml) hot stock or water
8 ounces (200 g) hazelnuts, roasted and chopped finely
⅛ pint (75 ml) hazelnut oil
oil
seasoning

Place the snipe in a roasting dish, season and rub with oil. Roast in a hot oven (400°F/205°C/gas regulo 6) for 10-12 minutes. Remove to a serving dish and keep warm.

Melt the butter in a saucepan and fry the chopped onion gently until transparent. Add the bacon and cook for 2-3 minutes. Add the flour and cook for a few minutes before adding the stock. Bring to the boil, stirring well. Season, then add the hazelnuts and hazelnut oil. Simmer for a few minutes then taste to correct the seasoning.

Serve the snipe with chateau potatoes (shaped like a pheasant egg, boiled, then roasted), and seasonal vegetables.

Roast Snipe with Guava Sauce

TIME TO ALLOW: 45 minutes
SERVES 6

6 snipe
1 pint (600 ml) hot stock or water
1 pound (450 g) fresh guavas (or if unavailable, canned guavas)
seasoning
pinch of sugar
oil
1 ounce (25 g) cornflour, mixed with a little cold water

Place the snipe in a roasting dish, season, and rub with oil. Roast in a hot oven (400°F/205°C/gas regulo 6) for 10-15 minutes. Remove to a serving tray and keep warm.

Peel the guavas and add with the stock to the roasting tray. Simmer until tender, then purée guavas and stock in a blender. Return to the heat and season with salt, pepper and sugar. Bring to the boil, correct the seasoning, then thicken with cornflour.

Serve the snipe and sauce separately.

Skewered Snipe with Citrus Stuffing

TIME TO ALLOW: 30 minutes
SERVES 4

4 snipe
½ tablespoon orange zest, chopped
½ teaspoon lemon zest, chopped
4 slices white bread, diced
1 egg yolk
⅛ pint (75 ml) milk
4 segments of orange
4 rashers bacon
1 green pepper, de-seeded and cut into quarters
½ pint (300 ml) sour cream
2 spring onions, thinly sliced
oil
seasoning

Remove the insides of the birds and discard the stomachs. Fry the entrails in a little oil, adding the chopped livers and hearts. Season and continue to cook for a few minutes. Add the orange and lemon zests, bread, egg yolk and milk. Remove from heat and mix well. Divide the stuffing into four and place inside each snipe.

Roll an orange segment inside each bacon rasher. Taking a skewer for each snipe, thread the bacon and orange roll, then the snipe and lastly the green pepper. Place the skewers on a roasting tray and roast in a very hot oven (425°F/220°C/gas regulo 7) for 10-15 minutes. Remove from tray and keep warm.

Add the sour cream to the roasting tray juices, bring to the boil and taste to correct the seasoning.

Serve the snipe with the sauce spooned over and a garnish of cherry tomatoes, peeled and sautéed in oil, croquettes of sweet potatoes, and steamed green beans.

Grilled Snipe with Pears

TIME TO ALLOW: 45 minutes
SERVES 6

6 snipe
3 pears, peeled, cored and halved
1 ounce (25 g) butter
1 ounce (25 g) flour
1 pint (600 ml) hot stock or water
⅛ pint (75 ml) kruskovac (pear liqueur)
pinch of sugar
oil
seasoning

Cut the snipe through the back, removing the backbone. Flatten the snipe by gently hitting them with the palm of your hand. Rub with oil and season. Heat up the grill with the thermostat on high. Place the snipe rib-side up on a roasting dish on the shelf directly below the element and grill for 10 minutes. Turn the snipe to brown the other side, then add the pear halves and cook for 5 minutes. Remove to a serving dish and keep warm.

Melt the butter in a heavy-bottomed saucepan and add the flour. Cook for a few minutes. Remove from heat and add the hot stock. Return to heat and bring to the boil, stirring all the time. Season, add the kruskovac and a pinch of sugar. Taste to correct the seasoning and strain into a sauceboat to serve.

Arrange the snipe with a pear half on each plate and perhaps some home-made gnocchis.

Sautéed Snipe with Mixed Peppercorn Sauce

TIME TO ALLOW: 45 minutes
SERVES 6

6 snipe
1 onion, sliced
1 green pepper, de-seeded and sliced
2 teaspoons green peppercorns
1 tablespoon pink peppercorns
1 tablespoon prepared mild mustard
½ pint (300 ml) plain yoghurt
oil
seasoning
flour

Split the snipe into halves and dust with flour. Heat a heavy-bottomed frying pan, add a little oil and brown the snipe evenly all over. Remove and set aside.

Sauté the onions in the frying pan and when nearly tender add the green pepper, green and pink peppercorns and mustard. Blend, then slowly add the yoghurt. Season, then return the snipe to the pan and simmer gently until the snipe are tender, about 10 minutes.

Arrange the snipe carefully on a serving dish and serve the sauce from a sauceboat.

Chilled Snipe with Tuna Sauce

TIME TO ALLOW: 30 minutes
SERVES 6

6 snipe, roasted and split with the rib-cage removed
6 ounces (150 g) tuna meat
1 ounce (25 g) anchovy fillets
1 clove garlic, crushed
juice from 1 lemon
2 ounces (50 g) capers
½ pint (300 ml) well-flavoured mayonnaise

Mash the tuna, anchovy fillets and garlic to a smooth paste. Add the lemon juice and capers, then the mayonnaise.

Dress the snipe on a serving dish, or on separate plates and serve the sauce to one side of the snipe.

Snipe in Red Lettuce

TIME TO ALLOW: 1 hour
SERVES 3, or 6 entrées

6 snipe, cooked and boned
½ pint (300 ml) prepared roast gravy
1 red lettuce
2 cloves garlic, crushed
¼ pint (150 ml) oil

Chop the cooked meat into bite-sized pieces and mix with the gravy, adding seasoning if necessary.

Choose six well-formed leaves from the red lettuce and shred the rest to add to the snipe mixture. Divide the filling evenly among the six leaves, roll them up neatly and tuck the edges in. Place in a deep roasting dish, sprinkle with garlic and oil, cover with foil and heat through in a moderate oven (375°F/190°C/gas regulo 4-5) for 20 minutes.

WOODCOCK

HUNTING SEASON
1st September-31st January

Woodcock are a larger version of snipe and should be hung for up to a week before plucking and cooking. They are at their best in November and December. Like snipe they are roasted undrawn.

Woodcock are considered to be a special delicacy when cooked complete with all their innards (apart from the gizzard but including the brain).

Sautéed Woodcock with Peanut Sauce

TIME TO ALLOW: 1 hour
SERVES 6

6 woodcock
¼ pint (150 ml) soya sauce
1 ounce (25 g) fresh root ginger, finely diced
1 clove garlic, crushed
pinch chilli powder
¼ pint (150 ml) peanut oil
6 ounces (150 g) crunchy peanut butter

Place the woodcock in a roasting dish with the soya sauce, ginger, garlic, chilli powder, and peanut oil. Mix thoroughly and allow to permeate for about 30 minutes, then roast in a very hot oven (450°F/230°C/gas regulo 8) for 5-6 minutes. Remove from oven and keep warm.

Add the peanut butter to the roasting tray juices, thinning with water if necessary. Return the woodcock to the dish and braise in a moderate oven (375°F/190°C/gas regulo 4-5) for a further 5 minutes so the flavour goes through the birds. Place the woodcock on a serving dish and coat with the sauce to serve.

Roast Woodcock

TIME TO ALLOW: 30-45 minutes
SERVES 6

6 woodcock
6 slices salt pork, or fatty bacon
seasoning
oil

Clean the woodcock, reserving the livers. Season the livers and place them inside the woodcock. Rub the woodcock with oil and season lightly. Wrap a slice of salt pork (or bacon) around each bird and roast in a moderately hot oven (400°F/205°C/gas regulo 6) for 25 minutes, or until tender.
   A rich roast gravy would be most suitable for this dish.

Flambéed Woodcock

TIME TO ALLOW: 30 minutes
SERVES 6

6 woodcock
⅛ pint (75 ml) brandy
½ pint (300 ml) white wine
6 rashers bacon
oil
seasoning

Clean the woodcock and reserve the intestines. Wrap the woodcock in a slice of bacon and roast for 5-6 minutes in a very hot oven (450°F/230°C/gas regulo 8). Remove from oven and cut each bird into 2 legs and 2 breasts.
   Flame the pan residue with the brandy, then add the wine. Crush the intestines and add them to the pan. Bring to the boil, season, and return the woodcock to the pan. Taste to correct the seasoning, bring to the boil, then serve.

Roast Woodcock with Avocado Sauce

TIME TO ALLOW: 1 hour
SERVES 6

6 woodcock
2 cloves garlic, crushed
¼ pint (150 ml) white wine
½ pint (300 ml) stock (or water)
2 avocados
flour
oil
seasoning

Heat the oil in a roasting dish, then dust the woodcock with flour and brown them in the oil. Season with salt and freshly ground black pepper and half the crushed garlic. Roast in a very hot oven (450°F/230°C/gas regulo 8) for 6 to 8 minutes.

Remove the flesh of the avocado by cutting them in half and removing the stone. Using a spoon, ease out the fruit and dice neatly.

Add the wine and stock (or water) to the roasting dish and bring to the boil. Add the avocado and remaining garlic and season.

Continue to braise the woodcock for a further 5 minutes, then remove them to a serving tray and keep warm.

Taste the sauce to correct the seasoning, then spoon over the woodcock to serve.

INDEX